TALES OF THE
MERMAID TAVERN

BY

ALFRED NOYES

Author of "Drake," "Sherwood," "The Enchanted Island," etc.

ILLUSTRATED

NEW YORK
FREDERICK A. STOKES COMPANY
PUBLISHERS

April, 1913

ILLUSTRATIONS

I

A KNIGHT OF THE OCEAN-SEA

TO
EDMUND GOSSE
IN GRATEFUL RECOLLECTION OF
GREAT ENCOURAGEMENT

CONTENTS

TALES OF
THE MERMAID TAVERN

I

A KNIGHT OF THE OCEAN-SEA

UNDER that foggy sunset London glowed,
  Like one huge cob-webbed flagon of old wine.
And, as I walked down Fleet Street, the soft sky
Flowed thro' the roaring thoroughfares, transfused
Their hard sharp outlines, blurred the throngs of black
On either pavement, blurred the rolling stream
Of red and yellow busses, till the town
Turned to a golden suburb of the clouds.
And, round that mighty bubble of St. Paul's,
Over the up-turned faces of the street,
An air-ship slowly sailed, with whirring fans,
A voyager in the new-found realms of gold,
A shadowy silken chrysalis whence should break
What radiant wings in centuries to be.

So, wandering on, while all the shores of Time
Softened into Eternity, it seemed
A dead man touched me with his living hand,
A flaming legend passed me in the streets
Of London — laugh who will — that City of Clouds,

Where what a dreamer yet, in spite of all,
Is man, that splendid visionary child
Who sent his fairy beacon through the dusk,
On a blue bus before the moon was risen,—
This Night, at eight, The Tempest!

        Dreaming thus,
(Small wonder that my footsteps went astray!)
I found myself within a narrow street,
Alone. There was no rumour, near or far,
Of the long tides of traffic. In my doubt
I turned and knocked upon an old inn-door,
Hard by, an ancient inn of mullioned panes,
And crazy beams and over-hanging eaves:
And, as I knocked, the slowly changing west
Seemed to change all the world with it and leave
Only that old inn steadfast and unchanged,
A rock in the rich-coloured tides of time.

And, suddenly, as a song that wholly escapes
Remembrance, at one note, wholly returns,
There, as I knocked, memory returned to me.
I knew it all — the little twisted street,
The rough wet cobbles gleaming, far away,
Like opals, where it ended on the sky;
And, overhead, the darkly smiling face
Of that old wizard inn; I knew by rote
The smooth sun-bubbles in the worn green paint
Upon the doors and shutters.

There was one
Myself had idly scratched away one dawn,
One mad May-dawn, three hundred years ago,
When out of the woods we came with hawthorn boughs
And found the doors locked, as they seemed to-night.
Three hundred years ago — nay, Time was dead!
No need to scan the sign-board any more
Where that white-breasted siren of the sea
Curled her moon-silvered tail among such rocks
As never in the merriest seaman's tale
Broke the blue-bliss of fabulous lagoons
Beyond the Spanish Main.

And, through the dream,
Even as I stood and listened, came a sound
Of clashing wine-cups: then a deep-voiced song
Made the old timbers of the Mermaid Inn
Shake as a galleon shakes in a gale of wind
When she rolls glorying through the Ocean-sea.

SONG

I

Marchaunt Adventurers, chanting at the windlass,
  Early in the morning, we slipped from Plymouth Sound,
All for Adventure in the great New Regions,
  All for Eldorado and to sail the world around!
Sing! the red of sun-rise ripples round the bows again.
  Marchaunt Adventurers, O sing, we're outward bound,
All to stuff the sunset in our old black galleon,
  All to seek the merchandise that no man ever found.

[3]

Chorus: Marchaunt Adventurers!
                 Marchaunt Adventurers!

Marchaunt Adventurers, O, whither are ye bound?—
All for Eldorado and the great new Sky-line,
    All to seek the merchandise that no man ever found.

II

Marchaunt Adventurers, O, what'ull ye bring home again?—
    Woonders and works and the thunder of the sea!

Whom will ye traffic with?— The King of the Sunset!
    What shall be your pilot then?—A wind from Galilee.
Nay, but ye be marchaunts, will ye come back empty-
       handed?—
    Ay, we be marchaunts, though our gain we ne'er shall see.
Cast we now our bread upon the waste wild waters.
    After many days, it shall return with usury.

Chorus: Marchaunt Adventurers!
                 Marchaunt Adventurers!

What shall be your profit in the mighty days to be?—
Englande!— Englande!— Englande!— Englande!—
    Glory everlasting and the lordship of the sea!

And there, framed in the lilac patch of sky
That ended the steep street, dark on its light,
And standing on those glistering cobble-stones
Just where they took the sunset's kiss, I saw
A figure like foot-feathered Mercury,
Tall, straight and splendid as a sunset-cloud,
Clad in a crimson doublet and trunk-hose,
A rapier at his side; and, as he paused,

His long fantastic shadow swayed and swept
Against my feet.

        A moment he looked back,
Then swaggered down as if he owned a world
Which had forgotten — did I wake or dream? —
Even his gracious ghost!

        Over his arm
He swung a gorgeous murrey-coloured cloak
Of Ciprus velvet, caked and smeared with mud
As on the day when — did I dream or wake?
And had not all this happened once before? —
When he had laid that cloak before the feet
Of Gloriana! By that mud-stained cloak,
'Twas he! Our Ocean-Shepherd! Walter Raleigh!
He brushed me passing, and with one vigorous thrust
Opened the door and entered. At his heels
I followed — into the Mermaid! — through three yards
Of pitch-black gloom, then into an old inn-parlour
Swimming with faces in a mist of smoke
That up-curled, blue, from long Winchester pipes,
While — like some rare old picture, in a dream
Recalled — quietly listening, laughing, watching,
Pale on that old black oaken wainscot floated
One bearded oval face, young, with deep eyes,
Whom Raleigh hailed as "Will!"

        But as I stared
A sudden buffet from a brawny hand
Made all my senses swim, and the room rang
With laughter as upon the rush-strewn floor
My feet slipped and I fell. Then a gruff-voice
Growled over me — " Get up now, John-a-dreams,

[5]

Or else mine host must find another drawer!
Hast thou not heard us calling all this while?"
And, as I scrambled up, the rafters rang
With cries of "Sack! Bring me a cup of sack!
Canary! Sack! Malmsey! and Muscadel!"
I understood and flew. I was awake,
A leather-jerkined pot-boy to these gods,
A prentice Ganymede to the Mermaid Inn!

There, flitting to and fro with cups of wine
I heard them toss the Chrysomelan names
From mouth to mouth — Lyly and Peele and Lodge,
Kit Marlowe, Michael Drayton, and the rest,
With Ben, rare Ben, brick-layer Ben, who rolled
Like a great galleon on his ingle-bench.
Some twenty years of age he seemed; and yet
This young Gargantua with the bull-dog jaws,
The T, for Tyburn, branded on his thumb,
And grim pock-pitted face was growling tales
To Dekker that would fright a buccaneer,—
How in the fierce Low Countries he had killed
His man, and won that scar on his bronzed fist;
Was taken prisoner, and turned Catholick;
And, now returned to London, was resolved
To blast away the vapours of the town
With Boreas-throated plays of thunderous mirth.
"I'll thwack their Tribulation-Wholesomes, lad,
Their Yellow-faced Envies and lean Thorns-i'-the-Flesh,
At the *Black-friars Theatre,* or *The Rose,*
Or else *The Curtain.* Failing these, I'll find
Some good square inn-yard with wide galleries,

And windows level with the stage.   'Twill serve
My Comedy of Vapours; though, I grant,
For Tragedy a private House is best,
Or, just as Burbage tip-toes to a deed
Of blood, or, over your stable's black half-door,
Marked *Battlements* in white chalk, your breathless David
Glowers at the whiter Bathsheba within,
Some humorous coach-horse neighs a 'hallelujah'!
And the pit splits its doublets.   Over goes
The whole damned apple-barrel, and the yard
Is all one rough and tumble, scramble and scratch
Of prentices, green madams, and cut-purses
For half-chewed Norfolk pippins.   Never mind!
We'll build the perfect stage in Shoreditch yet.
And Will, there, hath half promised I shall write
A piece for his own company!   What d'ye think
Of *Venus and Adonis,* his first heir,
Printed last week?   A bouncing boy, my lad!
And he's at work on a Midsummer's Dream
That turns the world to fairyland! "

                                  All these
And many more were there, and all were young!
There, as I brimmed their cups, I heard the voice
Of Raleigh ringing across the smoke-wreathed room,—
" Ben, could you put a frigate on the stage,
I've found a tragedy for you.   Have you heard
The true tale of Sir Humphrey Gilbert? "

                                          " No! "

" Why, Ben, of all the tragical affairs
Of the Ocean-sea, and of that other Ocean

Where all men sail so blindly, and misjudge
Their friends, their charts, their storms, their stars, their
      God,
If there be truth in the blind crowder's song
I bought in Bread Street for a penny, this
Is the brief type and chronicle of them all.
Listen!" Then Raleigh sent these rugged rhymes
Of some blind crowder rolling in great waves
Of passion across the gloom. At each refrain
He sank his voice to a broad deep undertone,
As if the distant roar of breaking surf
Or the low thunder of eternal tides
Filled up the pauses of the nearer storm,
Storm against storm, a soul against the sea:—

A KNIGHT OF THE OCEAN-SEA

Sir Humphrey Gilbert, hard of hand,
    Knight-in-chief of the Ocean-sea,
Gazed from the rocks of his New Found Land
    And thought of the home where his heart would be.

He gazed across the wintry waste
    That weltered and hissed like molten lead,—
"He saileth twice who saileth in haste!
    I'll wait the favour of Spring," he said.

> *Ever the more, ever the more,*
> *He heard the winds and the waves roar!*
> *Thunder on thunder shook the shore.*

The yellow clots of foam went by
    Like shavings that curl from a ship-wright's plane,

[8]

Clinging and flying, afar and nigh,
  Shuddering, flying and clinging again.

A thousand bubbles in every one
  Shifted and shimmered with rainbow gleams;
But — had they been planets and stars that spun
  He had let them drift by his feet like dreams:

Heavy of heart was our Admirall,
  For, out of his ships,—and they were but three!—
He had lost the fairest and most tall,
  And — he was a Knight of the Ocean-sea.

      Ever the more, ever the more,
      He heard the winds and the waves roar!
      Thunder on thunder shook the shore.

Heavy of heart, heavy of heart,
  For she was a galleon mighty as May,
And the storm that ripped her glory apart
  Had stripped his soul for the winter's way;

And he was aware of a whisper blown
  From foc'sle to poop, from windward to lee,
That the fault was his, and his alone,
  And — he was a Knight of the Ocean-sea.

"Had he done that! Had he done this!"
  And yet his mariners loved him well;
But an idle word is hard to miss,
  And the foam hides more than the deep can tell.

[9]

And the deep had buried his best-loved books,
　　With many a hard-won chart and plan:
And a king that is conquered must see strange looks,
　　So bitter a thing is the heart of man!

And —" Who will you find to pay your debt?
　　For a venture like this is a costly thing!
Will they stake yet more, tho' your heart be set
　　On the mightier voyage you planned for the Spring? "

He raised his head like a Viking crowned,—
　　" I'll take my old flag to her Majestie,
And she will lend me ten thousand pound
　　To make her Queen of the Ocean-sea! "

　　　　Ever the more, ever the more,
　　　　He heard the winds and the waves roar!
　　　　Thunder on thunder shook the shore.

Outside — they heard the great winds blow!
　　Outside — the blustering surf they heard,
And the bravest there would ha' blenched to know
　　That they must be taken at their own word.

For the great grim waves were as molten lead
　　— And he had two ships who sailed with three!—
" And I sail not home till the Spring," he said,
　　" They are all too frail for the Ocean-sea."

But the trumpeter thought of an ale-house bench,
　　And the cabin-boy longed for a Devonshire lane,

And the gunner remembered a green-gowned wench,
　　And the foc'sle whisper went round again,—

"Sir Humphrey Gilbert is hard of hand,
　　But his courage went down with the ship, may-be,
And we wait for the Spring in a desert land,
　　For — *he is afraid of the Ocean-sea.*"

　　　　Ever the more, ever the more,
　　　　He heard the winds and the waves roar!
　　　　Thunder on thunder shook the shore.

He knew, he knew how the whisper went!
　　He knew he must master it, last or first!
He knew not how much or how little it meant;
　　But his heart was heavy and like to burst.

"Up with your sails, my sea-dogs all!
　　The wind has veered! And my ships," quoth he,
"They will serve for a British Admirall
　　Who is Knight-in-chief of the Ocean-sea!"

His will was like a North-east wind
　　That swept along our helmless crew;
But he would not stay on the *Golden Hind,*
　　For that was the stronger ship of the two.

"My little ship's-company, lads, hath passed
　　Perils and storms a-many with me!
Would ye have me forsake them at the last?
　　They'll need a Knight of the Ocean-sea!"

Ever the more, ever the more,
We heard the winds and the waves roar!
Thunder on thunder shook the shore.

Beyond Cape Race, the pale sun splashed
  The grim grey waves with silver light
Where, ever in front, his frigate crashed
  Eastward, for England and the night.

And still as the dark began to fall,
  Ever in front of us, running free,
We saw the sails of our Admiral!
  Leading us home through the Ocean-sea.

Ever the more, ever the more,
We heard the winds and the waves roar!
But he sailed on, sailed on before.

On Monday, at noon of the third fierce day
  A-board our *Golden Hind* he came,
With a trail of blood, marking his way
  On the salt wet decks as he walked half-lame.

For a rusty nail thro' his foot had pierced.
  " Come, master-surgeon, mend it for me;
Though I would it were changed for the nails that
    amerced
  The dying thief upon Calvary."

The surgeon bathed and bound his foot,
  And the master entreated him sore to stay;

But roughly he pulled on his great sea-boot
  With—" The wind is rising and I must away ! "

I know not why so little a thing,
  When into his pinnace we helped him down,
Should make our eye-lids prick and sting
  As the salt spray were into them blown,

But he called as he went—" Keep watch and steer
  By my lanthorn at night ! "   Then he waved his hand
With a kinglier watch-word, " We are as near
  To heaven, my lads, by sea as by land ! "

> *Ever the more, ever the more,*
> *We heard the gathering tempest roar!*
> *But he sailed on, sailed on before.*

Three hundred leagues on our homeward road,
  We strove to signal him, swooping nigh,
That he would ease his decks of their load
  Of nettings and fights and artillery.

And dark and dark that night 'gan fall,
  And high the muttering breakers swelled,
Till that strange fire which seamen call
  " Castor and Pollux," we beheld,

An evil sign of peril and death,
  Burning pale on the high main-mast;
But calm with the might of Gennesareth
  Our Admirall's voice went ringing past,

Clear thro' the thunders, far and clear,
   Mighty to counsel, clear to command,
Joyfully ringing, "We are as near
   To heaven, my lads, by sea as by land!"

      Ever the more, ever the more,
      We heard the rising hurricane roar!
      But he sailed on, sailed on before.

And over us fled the fleet of the stars,
   And, ever in front of us, far or nigh,
The lanthorn on his cross-tree spars
   Dipped to the Pit or soared to the Sky!

'Twould sweep to the lights of Charles's Wain,
   As the hills of the deep 'ud mount and flee,
Then swoop down vanishing cliffs again
   To the thundering gulfs of the Ocean-sea.

We saw it shine as it swooped from the height,
   With ruining breakers on every hand,
Then — a cry came out of the black mid-night,
   As near to heaven by sea as by land!

And the light was out! Like a wind-blown spark,
   All in a moment! And we — and we —
Prayed for his soul as we swept thro' the dark;
   For he was a Knight of the Ocean-sea.

      Over our fleets for evermore
      The winds 'ull triumph and the waves roar!
      But he sails on, sails on before!

Silence a moment held the Mermaid Inn,
Then Michael Drayton, raising a cup of wine,
Stood up and said,—" Since many have obtained
Absolute glory that have done great deeds,
But fortune is not in the power of man,
So they that, truly attempting, nobly fail,
Deserve great honour of the common-wealth.
Such glory did the Greeks and Romans give
To those that in great enterprises fell
Seeking the true commodity of their country
And profit to all mankind ; for, though they failed,
Being by war, death, or some other chance,
Hindered, their images were set up in brass,
Marble and silver, gold and ivory,
In solemn temples and great palace-halls,
No less to make men emulate their virtues
Than to give honour to their just deserts.
God, from the time that He first made the world,
Hath kept the knowledge of His Ocean-sea
And the huge Æquinoctiall Continents
Reserved unto this day. Wherefore I think
No high exploit of Greece and Rome but seems
A little thing to these Discoveries
Which our adventurous captains even now
Are making, out there, Westward, in the night,
Captains most worthy of commendation,
Hugh Willoughby — God send him home again
Safe to the Mermaid!— and Dick Chauncellor,
That excellent pilot. Doubtless this man, too,
Sir Humphrey Gilbert, was worthy to be made

Knight of the Ocean-sea. I bid you all
Stand up, and drink to his immortal fame!"

II

A COINER OF ANGELS

II

A COINER OF ANGELS

SOME three nights later, thro' the thick brown fog,
    A link-boy, dropping flakes of crimson fire,
Flared to the door and, through its glowing frame,
Ben Jonson and Kit Marlowe, arm in arm,
Swaggered into the Mermaid Inn and called
For red-deer pies.

          There, as they supped, I caught
Scraps of ambrosial talk concerning Will,
His *Venus and Adonis*.

          "Gabriel thought
'Twas wrong to change the old writers and create
A cold Adonis."

          —"Laws were made for Will,
Not Will for laws, since first he stole a buck
In Charlecote woods."

          —"Where never a buck chewed fern,"
Laughed Kit, "unless it chewed the fern seed, too,
And walked invisible."

          "Bring me some wine," called Ben,
And, with his knife thrumming upon the board,
He chanted, while his comrade munched and smiled.

I

Will Shakespeare's out like Robin Hood
    With his merry men all in green,

[19]

To steal a deer in Charlecote wood
  Where never a deer was seen.

II

He's hunted all a night of June,
  He's followed a phantom horn,
He's killed a buck by the light of the moon,
  Under a fairy thorn.

III

He's carried it home with his merry, merry band,
  There never was haunch so fine;
For this buck was born in Elfin-land
  And fed upon sops-in-wine.

IV

This buck had browsed on elfin boughs
  Of rose-marie and bay,
And he's carried it home to the little white house
  Of sweet Anne Hathaway.

V

"The dawn above your thatch is red!
  Slip out of your bed, sweet Anne!
I have stolen a fairy buck," he said,
  "The first since the world began.

VI

"Roast it on a golden spit,
  And see that it do not burn;

[20]

For we never shall feather the like of it
  Out of the fairy fern."

VII

She scarce had donned her long white gown
  And given him kisses four,
When the surly Sheriff of Stratford-town
  Knocked at the little green door.

VIII

They have gaoled sweet Will for a poacher;
  But squarely he fronts the squire,
With "When did you hear in your woods of a deer?
  Was it under a fairy briar?"

IX

Sir Thomas he puffs,—" If God thought good
  My water-butt ran with wine,
Or He dropt me a buck in Charlecote wood,
  I wot it is mine, not thine!"

X

"If you would eat of elfin meat,"
  Says Will, "you must blow up your horn!
Take your bow, and feather the doe
  That's under the fairy thorn!

XI

"If you would feast on elfin food,
  You've only the way to learn!

[21]

Take your bow and feather the doe
    That's under the fairy fern!"

XII

They're hunting high, they're hunting low,
    They're all away, away,
With horse and hound to feather the doe   -
    That's under the fairy spray!

XIII

Sir Thomas he raged!   Sir Thomas he swore!
    But all and all in vain;
For there never was deer in his woods before,
    And there never would be again!

And, as I brought the wine —" This is my grace,"
Laughed Kit, " Diana grant the jolly buck
That Shakespeare stole were toothsome as this pie."

He suddenly sank his voice,—" Hist, who comes here?
Look — Richard Bame, the Puritan! O, Ben, Ben,
Your Mermaid Inn's the study for the stage,
Your only teacher of exits, entrances,
And all the shifting comedy. Be grave!
Bame is the godliest hypocrite on earth!
Remember I'm an atheist, black as coal.
He has called me Wormall in an anagram.
Help me to bait him; but be very grave.
We'll talk of Venus."
                    As he whispered thus,
A long white face with small black-beaded eyes
Peered at him through the doorway. All too well,

[22]

Afterwards, I recalled that scene, when Bame,
Out of revenge for this same night, I guessed,
Penned his foul tract on Marlowe's tragic fate;
And, twelve months later, I watched our Puritan
Riding to Tyburn in the hangman's cart
For thieving from an old bed-ridden dame
With whom he prayed, at supper-time, on Sundays.

Like a conspirator he sidled in,
Clasping a little pamphlet to his breast,
While, feigning not to see him, Ben began:—

"Will's *Venus and Adonis*, Kit, is great,
A round, sound, full-blown piece of thorough work,
On a great canvas, coloured like one I saw
In Italy, by one — Titian! None of the toys
Of artistry your lank-haired losels turn,
Your Phyllida — Love-lies-bleeding — Kiss-me-Quicks,
Your fluttering Sighs and Mark-how-I-break-my-beats,
Begotten like this, whenever and how you list,
Your Moths of verse that shrivel in every taper;
But a sound piece of craftsmanship to last
Until the stars are out. 'Tis twice the length
Of Vergil's books — he's listening! Nay, don't look!—
Two hundred solid stanzas, think of that;
But each a square celestial brick of gold
Laid level and splendid. I've laid bricks and know
What thorough work is. If a storm should shake
The Tower of London down, Will's house would stand.
Look at his picture of the stallion,
Nostril to croup, that's thorough finished work!"

" 'Twill shock our Tribulation-Wholesomes, Ben!
Think of that kiss of Venus!   Deep, sweet, slow,
As the dawn breaking to its perfect flower
And golden moon of bliss; then slow, sweet, deep,
Like a great honeyed sunset it dissolves
Away!"

    A hollow groan, like a bass viol,
Resounded thro' the room.   Up started Kit
In feigned alarm —" What, Master Richard Bame,
Quick, Ben, the good man's ill. Bring him some wine!
Red wine for Master Bame, the blood of Venus
That stained the rose!"

      " White wine for Master Bame,"
Ben echoed, " Juno's cream that " . . . Both at once
They thrust a wine-cup to the sallow lips
And smote him on the back.
" Sirs, you mistake!" coughed Bame, waving his hands
And struggling to his feet,
      " Sirs, I have brought
A message from a youth who walked with you
In wantonness, aforetime, and is now
Groaning in sulphurous fires!"

      " Kit, that means hell!"
" Yea, sirs, a pamphlet from the pit of hell,
Written by Robert Greene before he died.
Mark what he styles it — *A Groatsworth of Wit
Bought with a Million of Repentance!*"

      " Ah,
Poor Rob was all his life-time either drunk,
Wenching, or penitent, Ben! Poor lad, he died
Young. Let me see now, Master Bame, you say

Rob Greene wrote this on earth before he died,
And then you printed it yourself in hell!"
"Stay, sir, I came not to this haunt of sin
To make mirth for Beëlzebub!"

                   "O, Ben,
That's you!"

            "'Swounds, sir, am I Beëlzebub?
Ogs-gogs!" roared Ben, his hand upon his hilt!
"Nay, sir, I signified the god of flies!
I spake out of the scriptures!" snuffled Bame
With deprecating eye.

           "I come to save
A brand that you have kindled at your fire,
But not yet charred, not yet so far consumed,
One Richard Cholmeley, who declares to all
He was persuaded to turn Atheist
By Marlowe's reasoning. I have wrestled with him,
But find him still so constant to your words
That only you can save him from the fire."
"Why, Master Bame," said Kit, "had I the keys
To hell, the damned should all come out and dance
A morrice round the Mermaid Inn to-night."
"Nay, sir, the damned are damned!"

                  "Come, sit you down!
Take some more wine! You'd have them all be damned
Except Dick Cholmeley. What must I unsay
To save him?" A quick eye-lid dropt at Ben.
"Now tell me, Master Bame!"

               "Sir, he derides
The books of Moses!"

            "Bame, do you believe?—

There's none to hear us but Beëlzebub —
Do you believe that we must taste of death
Because God set a foolish naked wench
Too near an apple-tree, how long ago?
Five thousand years? But there were men on earth
Long before that!" "Nay, nay, sir, if you read
The books of Moses . . ." "Moses was a juggler!"
"A juggler, sir, how, what!" "Nay, sir, be calm!
Take some more wine — the white, if that's too red!
I never cared for Moses!   Help yourself
To red-deer pie.   Good!
                              All the miracles
You say that he performed — why, what are they?
I know one Heriots, lives in Friday Street,
Can do much more than Moses!   Eat your pie
In patience, friend, the mouth of man performs
One good work at a time.   What says he, Ben?
The red deer stops his — what?   Sticks in his gizzard?
O — *led them through the wilderness!* No doubt
He did — for forty years, and might have made
The journey in six months.   Believe me, sir,
That is no miracle.   Moses gulled the Jews!
Skilled in the sly tricks of the Egyptians,
Only one art betrayed him.   Sir, his books
Are filthily written.   I would undertake —
If I were put to write a new religion—
A method far more admirable.   Eh, what?
Gruel in the vestibule? Interpret, Ben!
His mouth's too full!   O, *the New Testament!*
Why, there, consider, were not all the Apostles
Fishermen and base fellows, without wit

Or worth? "— again his eye-lid dropt at Ben.—
" The Apostle Paul alone had wit, and he
Was a most timorous fellow in bidding us
Prostrate ourselves to worldly magistrates
Against our conscience! I shall fry for this?
I fear no bug-bears or hob-goblins, sir,
And would have all men not to be afraid
Of roasting, toasting, pitch-forks, or the threats
Of earthly ministers, tho' their mouths be stuffed
With curses or with crusts of red-deer pie!
One thing I will confess — if I must choose —
Give me the Papists that can serve their God
Not with your scraps, but solemn ceremonies,
Organs, and singing men, and shaven crowns.
Your protestant is a hypocritical ass! "

" Profligate! You blaspheme! " Up started Bame,
A little unsteady now upon his feet,
And shaking his crumpled pamphlet over his head!

" Nay — if your pie be done, you shall partake
A second course. Be seated, sir, I pray.
We atheists will pay the reckoning!
I had forgotten that a Puritan
Will swallow Moses like a red-deer pie
Yet choke at a wax-candle! Let me read
Your pamphlet. What, 'tis half addressed to me!
Ogs-gogs! Ben! Hark to this — the Testament
Of poor Rob Greene would cut Will Shakespeare off
With less than his own Groatsworth! Hark to this! "

And there, unseen by them, a quiet figure
Entered the room and beckoning me for wine
Seated himself to listen, Will himself,
While Marlowe read aloud with knitted brows.
" ' *Trust them not; for there is an upstart crow*
Beautified with our feathers! '
                                        —O, he bids
All green eyes open:—' *And, being an absolute*
Johannes fac-totum is in his own conceit
The only Shake-scene in a country! ' "
                                        " Feathers ! "
Exploded Ben, " Why, come to that, he pouched
Your eagle's feather of blank verse, and lit
His Friar Bacon's little magic lamp
At the Promethean fire of Faustus. Jove,
It was a faëry buck, indeed, that Will
Poached in that green-wood."
                                        " Ben, see that you walk
Like Adam, naked! Nay, in nakedness
Adam was first. Trust me, you'll not escape
This calumny! Vergil is damned — he wears
A hen-coop round his waist, nicked in the night
From Homer! Plato is branded for a thief,
Why, he wrote Greek! And old Prometheus, too,
Who stole his fire from heaven!"
                                        " Who printed it? "
" Chettle! I know not why, unless he too
Be one of these same dwarfs that find the world
Too narrow for their jealousies. Ben, Ben,
I tell thee 'tis the dwarfs that find no world
Wide enough for their jostling, while the giants,

WILLIAM SHAKESPEARE

From a Painting in the Collection of the Duke of Somerset

The gods themselves, can in one tavern find
Room wide enough to swallow the wide heaven
With all its crowded solitary stars."

"Let me begin, then, lad, with swallowing this."
The voice of Shakespeare quietly broke in,
As laying a hand on either shoulder of Kit
He stood behind him in the gloom and smiled
Across the table at Ben, whose eyes still blazed
With boyhood's generous wrath. "Rob was a poet.
And had I known . . . no matter! I am sorry
He thought I wronged him. His heart's blood beats in this.
Look, where he says he dies forsaken, Kit!"
"Died drunk, more like," growled Ben. "And if he did,"
Will answered, "none was there to help him home,
Had not a poor old cobbler chanced upon him,
Dying in the streets, and taken him to his house,
And let him break his heart on his own bed.
Read his last words. You know he left his wife
And played the moth at tavern tapers, burnt
His wings and dropt into the mud. Read here,
His dying words to his forsaken wife,
Written in blood, Ben, blood. Read it, '*I charge thee,
Doll, by the love of our youth, by my soul's rest,
See this man paid! Had he not succoured me
I had died in the streets.*' How young he was to call
Thus on their poor dead youth, this withered shadow
That once was Robin Greene. He left a child —
See — in its face he prays her not to find
The father's, but her own. '*He is yet green
And may grow straight,*' so flickers his last jest,

[29]

Then out for ever. At the last he begged
A penny-pott of malmsey. In the bill,
All's printed now for crows and daws to peck,
You'll find four shillings for his winding sheet.
He had the poet's heart and God help all
Who have that heart and somehow lose their way
For lack of helm, souls that are blown abroad
By the great winds of passion, without power
To sway them, chartless captains. Multitudes ply
Trimly enough from bank to bank of Thames
Like shallow wherries, while tall galleons,
Out of their very beauty driven to dare
The uncompassed sea, founder in starless nights,
And all that we can say is —'They died drunk!'"

"I have it from veracious witnesses,"
Bame snuffled, "that the death of Robert Greene
Was caused by a surfeit, sir, of Rhenish wine
And pickled herrings. Also, sir, that his shirt
Was very foul, and while it was at wash
He lay i' the cobbler's old blue smock, sir!"

                                        "Gods,"
The voice of Raleigh muttered nigh mine ear,
"I had a dirty cloak once on my arm;
But a Queen's feet had trodden it! Drawer, take
Yon pamphlet, have it fried in cod-fish oil
And bring it hither. Bring a candle, too,
And sealing-wax! Be quick. The rogue shall eat it,
And then I'll seal his lips."
                              "No — not to-night,"

Kit whispered, laughing, " I've a prettier plan
For Master Bame."

                              " As for that scrap of paper,"
The voice of Shakespeare quietly resumed,
" Why, which of us could send his heart and soul
Thro' Caxton's printing-press and hope to find
The pretty pair unmangled. I'll not trust
The spoken word, no, not of my own lips,
Before the Judgment Throne against myself
Or on my own defence; and I'll not trust
The printed word to mirror Robert Greene.
See — here's another Testament, in blood,
Written, not printed, for the Mermaid Inn.
Rob sent it from his death-bed straight to me,
Read it. 'Tis for the Mermaid Inn alone;
And when 'tis read, we'll burn it, as he asks."

Then, from the hands of Shakespeare, Marlowe took
A little scroll, and, while the winds without
Rattled the shutters with their ghostly hands
And wailed among the chimney-tops, he read:—

            Greeting to all the Mermaid Inn
            From their old Vice and Slip of Sin,
            Greeting, Ben, to you, and you
            Will Shakespeare and Kit Marlowe, too.
            Greeting from your Might-have-been,
            Your broken sapling, Robert Greene.

            Read my letter — 'Tis my last,
            Then let Memory blot me out,

I would not make my maudlin past
A trough for every swinish snout.
First, I leave a debt unpaid,
It's all chalked up, not much all told,
For Bread and Sack. When I am cold,
Doll can pawn my Spanish blade
And pay mine host. She'll pay mine host!
But . . . I have chalked up other scores
In your own hearts, behind the doors,
Not to be paid so quickly. Yet,
O, if you would not have my ghost
Creeping in at dead of night,
Out of the cold wind, out of the wet,
With weeping face and helpless fingers
Trying to wipe the marks away,
Read what I can write, still write,
While this life within them lingers.
Let me pay, lads, let me pay.

Item, for a peacock phrase,
Flung out in a sudden blaze,
Flung out at his friend Shake-scene,
By this ragged Might-have-been,
This poor Jackdaw, Robert Greene.

Will, I knew it all the while!
And you know it — and you smile!
My quill was but a Jackdaw's feather,
While the quill that Ben, there, wields,
Fluttered down thro' azure fields,
From an eagle in the sun;

And yours, Will, yours, no earth-born thing,
A plume of rainbow-tinctured grain,
Dropt out of an angel's wing.
Only a Jackdaw's feather mine,
And mine ran ink, and Ben's ran wine,
And yours the pure Pierian streams.

But I had dreams, O, I had dreams!
Dreams, you understand me, Will;
And I fretted at the tether
That bound me to the lowly plain,
Gnawed my heart out, for I knew
Once, tho' that was long ago,
I might have risen with Ben and you
Somewhere near that Holy Hill
Whence the living rivers flow.
Let it pass. I did not know
One bitter phrase could ever fly
So far through that immortal sky
— Seeing all my songs had flown so low —
One envious phrase that cannot die
From century to century.

Kit Marlowe ceased a moment, and the wind,
As if indeed the night were all one ghost,
Wailed round the Mermaid Inn, then sent once more
Its desolate passion through the reader's voice:—

Some truth there was in what I said.
Kit Marlowe taught you half your trade;
And something of the rest you learned

From me,— but all you took you earned.
You took the best I had to give,
You took my clay and made it live;
And that — why that's what God must do! —
My music made for mortal ears
You flung to all the listening spheres.
You took my dreams and made them true.
And, if I claimed them, the blank air
Might claim the breath I shape to prayer.
I do not claim it! Let the earth
Claim the thrones she brings to birth.
Let the first shapers of our tongue
Claim whate'er is said or sung,
Till the doom repeal that debt
And cancel the first alphabet.
Yet when, like a god, you scaled
The shining crags where my foot failed;
When I saw my fruit of the vine
Foam in the Olympian cup,
Or in that broader chalice shine
Blood-red, a sacramental drink,
With stars for bubbles, lifted up,
Through the universal night,
Up to the celestial brink,
Up to that quintessential Light
Where God acclaimed you for the wine
Crushed from those poor grapes of mine;
O, you'll understand, no doubt,
How the poor vine-dresser fell,
How a pin-prick can let out
All the bannered hosts of hell,

[34]

Nay, a knife-thrust, the sharp truth —
I had spilt my wine of youth,
The Temple was not mine to build.
My place in the world's march was filled.

Yet — through all the years to come —
Men to whom my songs are dumb
Will remember them and me
For that one cry of jealousy,
That curse where I had come to bless,
That harsh voice of unhappiness.
They'll note the curse, but not the pang,
Not the torment whence it sprang,
They'll note the blow at my friend's back,
But not the soul stretched on the rack.
They'll note the weak convulsive sting,
Not the crushed body and broken wing.

Item,— for my thirty years, 68138
Dashed with sun and splashed with tears,
Wan with revel, red with wine,
This Jack-o-lanthorn life of mine.
Other wiser, happier men,
Take the full three-score-and-ten,
Climb slow, and seek the sun.
Dancing down is soon done.
Golden boys, beware, beware,—
The ambiguous oracles declare
Loving gods for those that die
Young, as old men may; but I,
Quick as was my pilgrimage,
Wither in mine April age.

[35]

Item,— one groatsworth of wit,
Bought at an exceeding price,
Ay, a million of repentance.
Let me pay the whole of it.
Lying here these deadly nights,
Lads, for me the Mermaid lights
Gleam as for a castaway
Swept along a midnight sea
The harbour-lanthorns, each a spark,
A pin-prick in the solid dark,
That lets trickle through a ray
Glorious out of Paradise,
To stab him with new agony.
Let me pay, lads, let me pay!
Let the Mermaid pass the sentence:
I am pleading guilty now,
A dead leaf on the laurel-bough,
And the storm whirls me away.

Kit Marlowe ceased; but not the wailing wind
That round and round the silent Mermaid Inn
Wandered, with helpless fingers trying the doors,
Like a most desolate ghost.

                    A sudden throng
Of players bustled in, shaking the rain
From their plumed hats. "Veracious witnesses,"
The snuffle of Bame arose anew, " declare
It was a surfeit killed him, Rhenish wine
And pickled herrings. His shirt was very foul.
He had but one. His doublet, too, was frayed,
And his boots broken . . ."

                  " What! Gonzago, you!"
A short fat player called in a deep voice
Across the room and, throwing aside his cloak
To show the woman's robe he wore beneath,
Minced up to Bame and bellowed—" 'Tis such men
As you that tempt us women to our fall!"
And all the throng of players rocked and roared,
Till at a nod and wink from Kit a hush
Held them again.

               " Look to the door," he said,
" Is any listening?"   The young player crept,
A mask of mystery, to the door and peeped.
" All's well! The coast is clear!"

                       " Then shall we tell
Our plan to Master Bame?"

                    Round the hushed room
Went Kit, a pen and paper in his hand,
Whispering each to read, digest, and sign,
While Ben re-filled the glass of Master Bame.
" And now," said Kit aloud, " what think you, lads?
Shall he be told?"   Solemnly one or two
'Gan shake their heads with " Safety! safety! Kit!"
" O, Bame can keep a secret! Come, we'll tell him!
He can advise us how a righteous man
Should act! We'll let him share an he approve.
Now, Master Bame,— come closer — my good friend,
Ben Jonson here, hath lately found a way
Of — hush! Come closer!— coining money, Bame."
" Coining!" " Ay, hush, now! Hearken! A certain
    sure,
And indiscoverable method, sir!

He is acquainted with one Poole, a felon
Lately released from Newgate, hath great skill
In mixture of metals — hush! — and, by the help
Of a right cunning maker of stamps, we mean
To coin French crowns, rose-nobles, pistolettes,
Angels and English shillings."

                                  For one breath
Bame stared at him with bulging beetle-eyes,
Then murmured shyly as a country maid
In her first wooing, "It's not against the law?"
"Why, sir, who makes the law? Why should not Bame
Coin his own crowns like Queen Elizabeth?
She is but mortal! And consider, too,
The good works it should prosper in your hands,
Without regard to red-deer pies and wine
White as the Milky Way. Such secrets, Bame,
Were not good for the general; but a few
Discreet and righteous palms, your own, my friend,
And mine,— what think you?"

                            With a hesitant glance
Of well-nigh child-like cunning, screwing his eyes,
Bame laughed a little huskily and looked round
At that grave ring of anxious faces, all
Holding their breath and thrilling his blunt nerves
With their stage-practice. "And no risk?" breathed Bame,
"No risk at all?" "O, sir, no risk at all!
We make the very coins. Besides, that part
Touches not you. Yours is the honest face,
That's all we want."

                         "Why, sir, if you be sure
There is no risk . . ."

                              "You'll help to spend it. Good!
We'll talk anon of this, and you shall carry
More angels in your pocket, master Bame,
Then e'er you'll meet in heaven. Set hand on seal
To this now, master Bame, to prove your faith.
Come, all have signed it. Here's the quill, dip, write.
Good!"

                  And Kit, pocketing the paper, bowed
The gull to the inn-door, saying as he went,—
"You shall hear further when the plan's complete.
But there's one great condition — not one word,
One breath of scandal more on Robert Greene.
He's dead; but he was one of us. The day
You air his shirt, I air this paper, too."
No gleam of understanding, even then,
Illumed that long white face: no stage, indeed,
Has known such acting as the Mermaid Inn
That night, and Bame but sniggered, "Why, of course,
There's good in all men; and the best of us
Will make mistakes."

                        "But no mistake in this,"
Said Kit, "or all together we shall swing
At Tyburn — who knows what may leap to light? —
You understand? No scandal!" "Not a breath!"
So, in dead silence, Master Richard Bame
Went out into the darkness and the night,
To ask, as I have heard, for many a moon,
The price of malmsey-butts and silken hose,
And doublets slashed with satin.

                              As the door
Slammed on his back, the pent-up laughter burst

With echo and re-echo round the room,
But ceased as Will tossed on the glowing hearth
The last poor Testament of Robert Greene.
All watched it burn. The black wind wailed and moaned
Around the Mermaid as the sparks flew up.
" God, what a night for ships upon the sea,"
Said Raleigh, peering through the wet black panes,
" Well — we may thank Him for the Little Red Ring!"
" *The Little Red Ring,*" cried Kit, " *the Little Red Ring!*"
Then up stood Dekker on the old black settle.
" Give it a thumping chorus, lads," he called,
And sang this brave song of the Mermaid Inn:—

I

Seven wise men on an old black settle,
   Seven wise men of the Mermaid Inn,
Ringing blades of the one right metal,
   What is the best that a blade can win?
Bread and cheese, and a few small kisses?
   Ha! ha! ha! Would you take them — you?
— Ay, if Dame Venus would add to her blisses
   A roaring fire and a friend or two!

Chorus: Up now, answer me, tell me true!—
   — Ay, if the hussy would add to her blisses
   A roaring fire and a friend or two!

II

What will you say when the world is dying?
   What, when the last wild midnight falls

Dark, too dark for the bat to be flying
   Round the ruins of old St. Paul's?
What will be last of the lights to perish?
   What but the little red ring we knew,
Lighting the hands and the hearts that cherish
   A fire, a fire, and a friend or two!

Chorus: Up now, answer me, tell me true!
What will be last of the stars to perish?
   — The fire that lighteth a friend or two!

III

Up now, answer me, on your mettle
   Wisest man of the Mermaid Inn,
Soberest man on the old black settle,
   Out with the truth!   It was never a sin.—
Well, if God saved me alone of the seven,
   Telling me *you* must be damned, or *you,*
"This," I would say, "This is hell, not heaven!
   Give me the fire and a friend or two!"

Chorus: Steel was never so ringing true:
"God," we would say, "this is hell, not heaven!
   Give us the fire, and a friend or two!"

III

BLACK BILL'S HONEY-MOON

III

BLACK BILL'S HONEY-MOON

THE garlands of a Whitsun ale were strewn
       About our rushes, the night that Raleigh brought
Bacon to sup with us. There, on that night,
I saw the singer of the *Faërie Queen*
Quietly spreading out his latest cantos
For Shakespeare's eye, like white sheets in the sun.
Marlowe, our morning-star and Michael Drayton
Talked in that ingle-nook. And Ben was there,
Humming a song upon that old black settle:
           "Or leave a kiss but in the cup
              And I'll not ask for wine."
But, meanwhile, he drank malmsey.

                                    Francis Bacon
Straddled before the fire; and, all at once,
He said to Shakespeare, in a voice that gripped
The Mermaid Tavern like an arctic frost:
"There are no poets in this age of ours,
Not to compare with Plautus. They are all
Dead, the men that were famous in old days."
"Why — so they are," said Will. The humming stopped.
I saw poor Spenser, a shy gentle soul,
With haunted eyes like starlit forest pools,
Smuggling his cantos under his cloak again.

" There's verse enough, no doubt," Bacon went on,
" But English is no language for the Muse.
Whom would you call our best? There's Gabriel Harvey,
And Edward, Earl of Oxford. Then there's Dyer,
And Doctor Golding; while, for tragedy,
Thomas, Lord Buckhurst, hath a lofty vein.
And, in a lighter prettier vein, why, Will,
There is *thyself!* But — where's Euripides? "

" Dead," echoed Ben, in a deep ghost-like voice.
And drip — drip — drip — outside we heard the rain
Miserably dropping round the Mermaid Inn.

" Thy Summer's Night — eh, Will? Midsummer's Night?—
That's a quaint fancy," Bacon droned anew,
" But — Athens was an error, Will! Not Athens!
Titania knew not Athens! Those wild elves
Of thy Midsummer's Dream — eh? Midnight's Dream?—
Are English all. Thy woods, too, smack of England;
They never grew round Athens. Bottom, too,
He is not Greek! "
                              " Greek? " Will said, with a chuckle,
" Bottom a Greek? Why, no, he was the son
Of Marian Hacket, the fat wife that kept
An ale-house, Wincot-way. I lodged with her
Walking from Stratford. You have never tramped
Along that country side? By Burton Heath?
Ah, well, you would not know my fairy-lands.
It warms my blood to let my home-spuns play
Around your cold white Athens. There's a joy
In jumping time and space."

[46]

SIR FRANCIS BACON

From an Old Print

                              But, as he took
The cup of sack I proffered, solemnly
The lawyer shook his head. "Will, couldst thou use
Thy talents with discretion, and obey
Classic examples, thou mightst match old Plautus,
In all except priority of the tongue.
This English tongue is only for an age,
But Latin for all time. So I propose
To embalm in Latin my philosophies.
Well-seize your hour! But, ere you die, you'll sail
A British galleon to the golden courts
Of Cleopatra."

                    "Sail it!" Marlowe roared,
Mimicking in a fit of thunderous glee
The drums and trumpets of his Tamburlaine:
"And let her buccaneers bestride the sphinx,
And play at bowls with Pharaoh's pyramids,
And hale white Egypt with their tarry hands
Home to the Mermaid! Lift the good old song
That Rob Greene loved. Gods, how the lad would shout it!
Stand up and sing, John Davis!"

                              "Up!" called Raleigh,
"Lift the chanty of Black Bill's Honey-moon, Jack!
We'll keep the chorus going!"

                              "Silence, all!"
Ben Jonson echoed, rolling on his bench:
"This gentle lawyer hath a longing, lads,
To hear a right Homeric hymn. Now, Jack!
But wet your whistle, first! A cup of sack
For the first canto! Muscadel, the next!
Canary for the last!" I brought the cup.

John Davis emptied it at one mighty draught,
Leapt on a table, stamped with either foot,
And straight began to troll this mad sea-tale:

CANTO THE FIRST

Let Martin Parker at hawthorn-tide
    Prattle in Devonshire lanes,
Let all his pedlar poets beside
    Rattle their gallows-chains,
A tale like mine they never shall tell
    Or a merrier ballad sing,
Till the Man in the Moon pipe up the tune
    And the stars play Kiss-in-the-Ring!

Chorus: Till Philip of Spain in England reign,
    And the stars play Kiss-in-the-Ring!

All in the gorgeous dawn of day
    From grey old Plymouth Sound
Our galleon crashed thro' the crimson spray
    To sail the world around:
Cloud i' the Sun was her white-scrolled name,—
    There was never a lovelier lass
For sailing in state after pieces of eight
    With her bombards all of brass.

Chorus: Culverins, robinets, iron may-be;
    But her bombards all of brass!

Now, they that go down to the sea in ships,
    Though piracy be their trade,

[48]

For all that they pray not much with their lips
    They know where the storms are made:
With the stars above and the sharks below,
    They need not parson or clerk;
But our bo'sun Bill was an atheist still,
    Except — sometimes — in the dark!

Chorus: Now let Kit Marlowe mark!
    Our bo'sun Bill was an atheist still,
        Except — sometimes — in the dark!

All we adventured for, who shall say,
    Nor yet what our port might be?—
A magical city of old Cathay,
    Or a castle of Muscovy,
With our atheist bo'sun, Bill, Black Bill,
    Under the swinging Bear,
Whistling at night for a seaman to light
    His little poop-lanthorns there.

Chorus: On the deep, in the night, for a seaman to light
    His little lost lanthorns there.

But, as over the Ocean-sea we swept,
    We chanced on a strange new land
Where a valley of tall white lilies slept
    With a forest on either hand;
A valley of white in a purple wood
    And, behind it, faint and far,
Breathless and bright o'er the last rich height,
    Floated the sunset-star.

Chorus: Fair and bright o'er the rose-red height,
            Venus, the sunset-star.

'Twas a marvel to see, as we beached our boat,
   Black Bill, in that peach-bloom air,
With the great white lilies that reached to his
      throat
   Like a stained-glass bo'sun there,
And our little ship's chaplain, puffing and red,
   A-starn as we onward stole,
With the disk of a lily behind his head
   Like a cherubin's aureole.

Chorus: He was round and red and behind his head
            He'd a cherubin's aureole.

" Hyrcania, land of honey and bees,
   We have found thee at last," he said,
" Where the honey-comb swells in the hollow
      trees,"
   (O, the lily behind his head!)
" The honey-comb swells in the purple wood!
   'Tis the swette which the heavens distil,
Saith Pliny himself, on my little book-shelf!
   Is the world not sweet to thee, Bill? "

Chorus: " Saith Pliny himself, on my little book-shelf!
            Is the world not sweet to thee, Bill? "

Now a man may taste of the devil's hot spice,
   And yet if his mind run back

To the honey of childhood's Paradise
    His heart is not wholly black;
And Bill, Black Bill, from the days of his youth,
    Tho' his chest was broad as an oak,
Had cherished one innocent little sweet tooth,
    And it itched as our chaplain spoke.

Chorus: He had kept one perilous little tooth,
    And it itched as our Chaplain spoke.

All around was a mutter of bees,
    And Bill 'gan muttering too,—
"If the honey-comb swells in the hollow trees,
    (What else can a Didymus do?)
I'll steer to the purple woods myself
    And see if this thing be so,
Which the chaplain found on his little book-shelf,
    For Pliny lived long ago."

Chorus: There's a platter of delf on his little book-shelf,
    And Pliny lived long ago.

Scarce had he spoken when, out of the wood,
    And buffeting all around,
Rooting our sea-boots where we stood,
    There rumbled a marvellous sound,
As a mountain of honey were crumbling asunder,
    Or a sunset-avalanche hurled
Honey-comb boulders of golden thunder
    To smother the old black world.

[51]

Chorus: Honey-comb boulders of musical thunder
            To mellow this old black world.

And the chaplain he whispered —"This honey,
     one saith,
     On my camphired cabin-shelf,
None may harvest on pain of death;
     For the bee would eat it himself!
None walketh those woods but him whose voice
     In the dingles you then did hear!"
"A VOICE?" growls Bill! "Ay, Bill, r-r-rejoice!
     'Twas the great Hyrcanian Bear!"

Chorus: Give thanks! *Re*-joice! 'Twas the glor-r-r-ious
            Voice
            Of the great Hyrcanian Bear!

But, marking that Bill looked bitter indeed,
     For his sweet tooth hungered sore,
"Consider," he saith, "that the Sweet hath need
     Of the Sour, as the Sea of the Shore!
As the night to the day is our grief to our joy,
     And each for its brother prepares
A banquet, Bill, that would otherwise cloy.
     Thus is it with honey and bears."

Chorus: Roses and honey and laughter would cloy!
            Give us thorns, too, and sorrow and bears!

"Consider," he saith, "how by fretting a string
     The lutanist maketh sweet moan,

And a bird ere it fly must have air for its wing
    To buffet or fall like a stone:
Tho' you blacken like Pluto you make but more
    white
    These blooms which not Enna could yield!
Consider, Black Bill, ere the coming of night,
    The lilies," he saith, " of the field."

Chorus: " Consider, Black Bill, in this beautiful light,
      The lilies," he saith, " of the field."

" Consider the claws of a Bear," said Bill,
    " That can rip off the flesh from your bones,
While his belly could cabin the skipper and still
    Accommodate Timothy Jones!
Why, that's where a seaman who cares for his grog
    Perspires how this world isn't square!
If there's *cause* for a *cow,* if there's *use* for a *dog,*
    By Pope John, there's no *Sense* in a *Bear!* "

Chorus: Cause for a cow, use for a dog,
      By'r Lakin, no *Sense* in a *Bear!*

But our little ship's chaplain —" Sense," quoth he,
    " Hath the Bear tho' his making have none;
For, my little book saith, by the sting of this bee
    Would Ursus be wholly foredone,
But, or ever the hive he adventureth nigh
    And its crisp gold-crusted dome,
He lardeth his nose and he greaseth his eye
    With a piece of an honey-comb."

Chorus: His velvety nose and his sensitive eye
       With a piece of an honey-comb.

Black Bill at the word of that golden crust
    — For his ears had forgotten the roar,
And his eyes grew soft with their innocent lust —
    'Gan licking his lips once more:
" Be it bound like a missal and printed as fair,
    With capitals blue and red,
'Tis a lie; for what honey could comfort a bear,
    Till the bear win the honey? " he said.

Chorus: " Ay, *whence* the first honey wherewith the first
          bear
       First larded his nose? " he said.

" Thou first metaphysical bo'sun, Bill,"
    Our chaplain quizzingly cried,
" Wilt thou riddle me redes of a dumpling still
    With thy ' how came the apple inside '? "
" Nay," answered Bill, " but I quest for truth,
    And I find it not on your self!
I will face your Hyrcanian bear, forsooth,
    And look at his nose myself."

Chorus: For truth, for truth, or a little sweet tooth —
       I will into the woods myself.

Breast-high thro' that foam-white ocean of bloom
    With its wonderful spokes of gold,
Our sun-burnt crew in the rose-red gloom
    Like buccaneer galleons rolled:

[54]

Breast-high, breast-high in the lilies we stood,
   And before we could say " good-night,"
Out of the valley and into the wood
   He plunged thro' the last rich light.

Chorus: Out of the lilies and into the wood,
      Where the Great Bear walks all night!

And our little ship's chaplain he piped thro' the
     trees
   As the moon rose, white and still,
" Hylas, return to thy Heracles!"
   And we helped him with " Come back, Bill!"
Thrice he piped it, thrice we halloo'd,
   And thrice we were dumb to hark;
But never an answer came from the wood,
   So — we turned to our ship in the dark.

Chorus: Good-bye, Bill! you're a Didymus still;
      But — you're all alone in the dark.

" This honey now " — as the first canto ceased,
The great young Bacon pompously began —
" Which Pliny calleth, as it were, the swette
Of heaven, or spettle of the stars, is found
In Muscovy. Now . . ." " Bring the muscadel,"
Ben Jonson roared —" 'Tis a more purple drink,
And suits with the next canto!"

                    At one draught
John Davis drained the cup, and with one hand
Beating the measure, rapidly trolled again.

CANTO THE SECOND

Now, Rabelais, art thou quite foredone,
Dan Chaucer, Drayton, Every One!
Leave we aboard our *Cloud i' the Sun*
   This crew of pirates dreaming —
Of Angels, minted in the blue
Like golden moons, Rose-nobles, too,
As under the silver-sliding dew
   Our emerald creek lay gleaming!

Chorus: Under the stars lay gleaming!

And mailed with scales of gold and green
The high star-lilied banks between,
Nosing our old black hulk unseen,
   Great alligators shimmered:
Blood-red jaws i' the blue-black ooze,
Where all the long warm day they snooze,
Chewing old cuds of pirate-crews,
   Around us grimly glimmered.

Chorus: Their eyes like rubies glimmered.

Let us now sing of Bill, good sirs!
Follow him, all green forestéres,
Fearless of Hyrcanian bears
   As of these ghostly lilies!
For O, not Drayton there could sing
Of wild Pigwiggen and his King
So merry a jest, so jolly a thing
   As this my tale of Bill is.

[56]

BLACK BILL'S HONEY-MOON

Chorus: Into the woods where Bill is!

Now starts he as a white owl hoots,
And now he stumbles over roots,
And now beneath his big sea-boots
   In yon deep glade he crunches
Black cakes of honey-comb that were
So elfin-sweet, perchance, last year;
But neither Bo'sun, now, nor Bear
   At that dark banquet munches.

Chorus: Onward still he crunches!

Black cakes of honey-comb he sees
Above him in the forks of trees,
Filled by stars instead of bees,
   With brimming silver glisten:
But ah, such food of gnome and fay
Could neither Bear nor Bill delay
Till where yon ferns and moon-beams play
   He starts and stands to listen!

Chorus: What melody doth he listen?

Is it the Night-Wind as it comes
Through the wood and softly thrums
Silvery tabors, purple drums,
   To speed some wild-wood revel?
Nay, Didymus, what faint sweet din
Of viol and flute and violin
Makes all the forest round thee spin,
   The Night-Wind or the Devil?

[57]

Chorus: No doubt at all — the Devil!

He stares, with naked knife in hand,
This buccaneer in fairyland!
Dancing in a saraband
    The red ferns reel about him!
Dancing in a morrice-ring
The green ferns curtsey, kiss and cling!
Their Marions flirt, their Robins fling
    Their feathery heels to flout him!

Chorus: The whole wood reels about him.

Dance, ye shadows! O'er the glade,
Bill, the Bo'sun, undismayed,
Pigeon-toes with glittering glade!
    Drake was never bolder!
Devil or Spaniard, what cares he
Whence your eerie music be?
Till — lo, against yon old oak-tree
    He leans his brawny shoulder!

Chorus: He lists and leans his shoulder!

Ah, what melody doth he hear
As to that gnarled old tree-trunk there
He lays his wind-bit brass-ringed ear,
    And steals his arm about it?
What Dryad could this Bo'sun win
To that slow-rippling amorous grin?—
'Twas full of singing bees within!
    Not Didymus could doubt it!

Chorus: So loud they buzzed about it!

Straight, o'er a bough one leg he throws,
And up that oaken main-mast goes
With reckless red unlarded nose
   And goose-berry eyes of wonder!
Till now, as in a galleon's hold,
Below, he sees great cells of gold
Whence all the hollow trunk up-rolled
   A low melodious thunder.

Chorus: A sweet and perilous thunder!

Ay, there, within that hollow tree,
Will Shakespeare, might'st thou truly see
The Imperial City of the Bee,
   In Chrysomelan splendour!
And, in the midst, one eight-foot dome
Swells o'er that Titan honey-comb
Where the Bee-Empress hath her home,
   With such as do attend her.

Chorus: Weaponed with stings attend her!

But now her singing sentinels
Have turned to sleep in waxen cells,
And Bill leans down his face and smells
   The whole sweet summer's cargo —
In one deep breath, the whole year's bloom,
Lily and thyme and rose and broom,
One Golden Fleece of flower-perfume
   In that old oaken Argo.

Chorus: That green and golden Argo!

And now he hangs with dangling feet
Over that dark abyss of sweet,
Striving to reach such wild gold meat
    As none could buy for money:
His left hand grips a swinging branch
When — crack! Our Bo'sun, stout and stanch,
Falls like an Alpine avalanche,
    Feet first into the honey!

Chorus: Up to his ears in honey!

And now his red un-larded nose
And bulging eyes are all that shows
Above it, as he puffs and blows!
    And now — to 'scape the scathing
Of that black host of furious bees
His nose and eyes he fain would grease
And bobs below those golden seas
    Like an old woman bathing.

Chorus: Old Mother Hubbard bathing!

And now he struggles, all in vain,
To reach some little bough again;
But, though he heaves with might and main,
    This honey holds his ribs, sirs,
So tight, a barque might sooner try
To steer a cargo through the sky
Than Bill, thus honey-logged, to fly
    By flopping of his jib, sirs!

BLACK BILL'S HONEY-MOON

Chorus: His tops'l and his jib, sirs!

Like Oberon in the hive his beard
With wax and honey all besmeared
Would make the crescent moon afeard
   That now is sailing brightly
Right o'er his leafy donjon-keep!
But that she knows him sunken deep,
And that his tower is straight and steep,
   She would not smile so lightly.

Chorus: Look down and smile so lightly.

She smiles in that small heavenly space,
Ringed with the tree-trunk's leafy grace,
While upward grins his ghastly face
   As if some wid-wood Satyr,
Some gnomish Ptolemy should dare
Up that dark optic tube to stare,
As all unveiled she floated there,
   Poor maiden moon, straight at her!

Chorus: The buccaneering Stayr!

But there, till some one help him out,
Black Bill must stay, without a doubt.
"Help! Help!" he gives a muffled shout!
   None but the white owls hear it!
Who? Whoo? they cried: Bill answers " ME!
*I am stuck fast in this great tree!
Bring me a rope, good Timothy!
   There's honey, lads, we'll share it!"*

Chorus: Ay, now he wants to share it.

Then, thinking help may come with morn,
He sinks, half-famished and out-worn,
And scarce his nose exalts its horn
    Above that sea of glory!
But, even as he owns defeat,
His belly saith, " A man must eat,
And since there is none other meat,
    Come, lap this mess before 'ee!"

Chorus: This glorious mess before 'ee.

Then Dian sees a right strange sight
As, bidding him a fond good-night,
She flings a silvery kiss to light
    In that deep oak-tree hollow,
And finds that gold and crimson nose
A moving, munching, ravenous rose
That up and down unceasing goes,
    Save when he stops to swallow!

Chorus: He finds it hard to swallow!

Ay, now his best becomes his worst,
For honey cannot quench his thirst,
Though he should eat until he burst;
    But, ah, the skies are kindly,
And from their tender depths of blue
They send their silver-sliding dew.
So Bill thrusts out his tongue anew
    And waits to catch it — blindly!

Chorus: For ah, the stars are kindly!

And sometimes, with a shower of rain,
They strive to ease their prisoner's pain:
Then Bill thrusts out his tongue again
   With never a grace, the sinner!
And day and night and day goes by,
And never a comrade comes anigh,
And still the honey swells as high
   For supper, breakfast, dinner!

Chorus: Yet Bill has grown no thinner!

The young moon grows to full and throws
Her buxom kiss upon his nose,
As nightly over the tree she goes,
   And peeps and smiles and passes,
Then with her fickle silver flecks
Our old black galleon's dreaming decks;
And then her face, with nods and becks,
   In midmost ocean glasses.

Chorus: 'Twas ever the way with lasses!

Ah, Didymus, hast thou won indeed
That Paradise which is thy meed?
(Thy tale not all that run may read!)
   Thy sweet hath now no leaven!
Now, like an onion in a cup
Of mead, thou liest for Jove to sup,
Could Polyphemus lift thee up
   With Titan hands to heaven!

[63]

Chorus: This great oak-cup to heaven!

The second canto ceased; and, as they raised
Their wine-cups with the last triumphant note,
Bacon, undaunted, raised his grating voice —
"This honey which, in some sort, may be styled
The Spettle of the Stars . . ." "Bring the Canary!"
Ben Jonson roared. "It is a moral wine
And suits the third, last canto!" At one draught
John Davis drained it and began anew.

CANTO THE THIRD

A month went by. We were hoisting sail!
    We had lost all hope of Bill;
Though, laugh as you may at a seaman's tale,
    He was fast in his honey-comb still!
And often he thinks of the chaplain's word
    In the days he shall see no more,—
How the Sweet, indeed, of the Sour hath need;
    And the Sea, likewise, of the Shore.

Chorus: The chaplain's word of the Air and a Bird;
              Of the Sea, likewise, and the Shore!

"O, had I the wings of a dove, I would fly
    To a heaven, of aloes and gall!
I have honeyed," he yammers, "my nose and
        mine eye,
    And the bees cannot sting me at all!
And it's O, for the sting of a little brown bee,
    Or to blister my hands on a rope,

[64]

Or to buffet a thundering broad-side sea
    On a deck like a mountain-slope!"

Chorus: With her mast snapt short, and a list to port
    And a deck like a mountain-slope.

But alas, and he thinks of the chaplain's voice
    When that roar from the woods out-break —
R-r-re-joice! R-r-re-joice! Now, wherefore re-
    joice
    In the music a bear could make?
'Tis a judgment, maybe, that I stick in this tree;
    Yet in this I out-argued him fair!
Though I live, though I die, in this honey-comb
    pie,
    By Pope Joan, there's no sense in a bear!

Chorus: Notes in a nightingale, plums in a pie,
    By'r Lakin, no *Sense* in a *Bear!*

He knew not our anchor was heaved from the
    mud:
    He was growling it over again,
When — a strange sound suddenly froze his blood,
    And curdled his big slow brain!—
A marvellous sound, as of great steel claws
    Gripping the bark of his tree,
Softly ascended!   Like lightning ended
    His honey-comb reverie!

Chorus: The honey-comb quivered! The little leaves
    shivered!
    Something was climbing the tree!

Something that breathed like a fat sea-cook,
  Or a pirate of fourteen ton!
But it clomb like a cat (tho' the whole tree shook)
  Stealthily tow'rds the sun,
Till, as Black Bill gapes at the little blue ring
  Overhead, which he calls the sky,
It is clean blotted out by a monstrous Thing
  Which — *hath larded its nose and its eye.*

Chorus: O, well for thee, Bill, that this monstrous Thing
  Hath blinkered its little red eye.

Still as a mouse lies Bill with his face
  Low down in the dark sweet gold,
While this monster turns round in the leaf-
    fringed space!
  Then — taking a good firm hold,
As the skipper descending the cabin-stair,
  Tail-first with a vast slow tread,
Solemnly, softly, cometh this Bear
  Straight down o'er the Bo'sun's head.

Chorus: Solemnly — slowly — cometh this Bear,
  Tail-first o'er the Bo'sun's head.

Nearer — nearer — then all Bill's breath
  Out-bursts in one leap and yell!
And this Bear thinks, " Now am I gripped from
    beneath
  By a roaring devil from hell!"
And madly Bill clutches his brown bow-legs,
  And madly this Bear doth hale,

[66]

With his little red eyes fear-mad for the skies
And Bill's teeth fast in his tail!

Chorus: Small wonder a Bear should quail!
To have larded his nose, to have greased his eyes,
And be stung at the last in his tail.

Pull, Bo'sun! Pull, Bear! In the hot sweet gloom,
Pull Bruin, pull Bill, for the skies!
Pull — out of their gold with a bombard's boom
Come Black Bill's honeyed thighs!
Pull! Up! Up! Up! with a scuffle and scramble,
To that little blue ring of bliss,
This Bear doth go with our Bo'sun in tow
Stinging his tail, I wis.

Chorus: And this Bear thinks — " Many great bees I know,
But there never was Bee like this!"

   .   .   .   .

All in the gorgeous death of day
We had slipped from our emerald creek,
And our *Cloud i' the Sun* was careening away
With the old gay flag at the peak,
When, suddenly, out of the purple wood,
Breast-high thro' the lilies there danced
A tall lean figure, black as a nigger,
That shouted and waved and pranced!

Chorus: A gold-greased figure, but black as a nigger,
Waving his shirt as he pranced!

" 'Tis Hylas! 'Tis Hylas!" our chaplain flutes,
    And our skipper he looses a shout!
" 'Tis Bill! Black Bill, in his old sea-boats!
    Stand by to bring her about!
Har-r-rd a-starboard!" And round we came,
    With a lurch and a dip and a roll,
And a banging boom thro' the rose-red gloom
    For our old Black Bo'sun's soul!

Chorus: *Alive!* Not dead! Tho' behind his head
      He'd a seraphin's aureole!

.   .   .   .   .   .

And our chaplain he sniffs, as Bill finished his tale,
    (With the honey still scenting his hair!)
O'er a plate of salt beef and a mug of old ale—
    "By Pope John, there's no sense in a bear!"
And we laughed, but our Bo'sun he solemnly
      growls
    —"Till the sails of yon heavens be furled,
It taketh—now, mark!—all the beasts in the
      Ark,
    Teeth and claws, too, to make a good world!"

Chorus: Till the great—blue—sails—be—furled,
      It taketh—now, mark!—all the beasts in the
        Ark,
      Teeth and claws, too, to make a good world!

"Sack! Sack! Canary! Malmsey! Muscadel!"—
As the last canto ceased, the Mermaid Inn
Chorussed. I flew from laughing voice to voice;

But, over all the hubbub, rose the drone
Of Francis Bacon,—" Now, this Muscovy
Is a cold clime, not favourable to bees
(Or love, which is a weakness of the south)
As well might be supposed. Yet, as hot lands
Gender hot fruits and odoriferous spice,
In this case we may think that honey and flowers
Are comparable with the light airs of May
And a more temperate region. Also we see,
As Pliny saith, this honey being a swette
Of heaven, a certain spettle of the stars,
Which, gathering unclean vapours as it falls,
Hangs as a fat dew on the boughs, the bees
Obtain it partly thus, and afterwards
Corrupt it in their stomachs, and at last
Expel it through their mouths and harvest it
In hives; yet, of its heavenly source it keeps
A great part. Thus, by various principles
Of natural philosophy we observe —"
And, as he leaned to Drayton, droning thus,
I saw a light gleam of celestial mirth
Flit o'er the face of Shakespeare — scarce a smile —
A swift irradiation from within
As of a cloud that softly veils the sun.

IV

THE SIGN OF THE GOLDEN SHOE

IV

THE SIGN OF THE GOLDEN SHOE

WE had just set our brazier smouldering,
    To keep the Plague away.   Many a house
Was marked with the red cross.   The bells tolled
Incessantly.   Nash crept into the room
Shivering like a fragment of the night,
His face yellow as parchment, and his eyes
Burning.

            "The Plague!   He has taken it!" voices cried.
"That's not the Plague!   The old carrion-crow is drunk;
But stand away.   What ails you, Nash my lad?"
Then, through the clamour, as through a storm at sea,
The master's voice, the voice of Ben, rang out,
"Nash!"

            Ben leapt to his feet, and like a ship
Shouldering the waves, he shouldered the throng aside.
"What ails you, man?   What's that upon your breast?
Blood?"

            "Marlowe is dead," said Nash,
And stunned the room to silence. . . .

                            "Marlowe — dead!"
Ben caught him by the shoulders.   "Nash!   Awake!
What do you mean?   Marlowe?   Kit Marlowe?   Dead?
I supped with him — why — not three nights ago!
You are drunk!   You are dazed!   There's blood upon your
    coat!"

"That's — where he died," said Nash, and suddenly sank
Sidelong across a bench, bowing his head
Between his hands. . . .
Wept, I believe. Then, like a whip of steel,
His lean black figure sprang erect again.
"Marlowe!" he cried, "Kit Marlowe, killed for a punk,
A taffeta petticoat! Killed by an apple-squire!
Drunk! I was drunk; but I am sober now,
Sober enough, by God! Poor Kit is dead."

. . . .

The Mermaid Inn was thronged for many a night
With startled faces. Voices rose and fell,
As I recall them, in a great vague dream,
Curious, pitiful, angry, thrashing out
The tragic truth. Then, all along the Cheape,
The ballad-mongers waved their sheets of rhyme,
Croaking: *Come buy! Come buy! The bloody death
Of Wormall, writ by Master Richard Bame!
Come buy! Come buy! The Atheist's Tragedy.*
And, even in Bread Street, at our very door,
The crowder to his cracked old fiddle sang:—

> "*He was a poet of proud repute
> And wrote full many a play,
> Now strutting in a silken suit,
> Now begging by the way.*"

Then, out of the hubbub and the clash of tongues,
The bawdy tales and scraps of balladry,
(As out of chaos rose the slow round world)
At last, though for the Mermaid Inn alone,

Emerged some tragic semblance of a soul,
Some semblance of the rounded truth, a world
Glimpsed only through great mists of blood and tears,
Yet smitten, here and there, with dreadful light,
As I believe, from heaven.
                                    Strangely enough,
(Though Ben forgot his pipe and Will's deep eyes
Deepened and softened, when they spoke of Kit,
For many a month thereafter) it was Nash
That took the blow like steel into his heart.
Nash, our "Piers Penniless," whom Rob Greene had called
"Young Juvenal," the first satirist of our age,
Nash, of the biting tongue and subtle sneer,
Brooded upon it, till his grief became
Sharp as a rapier, ready to lunge in hate
At all the lies of shallower hearts.
                                    One night,
The night he raised the mists from that wild world,
He talked with Chapman in the Mermaid Inn
Of Marlowe's poem that was left half-sung,
His *Hero and Leander*.
                                    "Kit desired,
If he died first, that you should finish it,"
Said Nash.
                    A loaded silence filled the room
As with the imminent spirit of the dead
Listening. And long that picture haunted me:
Nash, like a lithe young Mephistopheles
Leaning between the silver candle-sticks,
Across the oak table, with his keen white face,
Dark smouldering eyes, and black, dishevelled hair;

Chapman, with something of the steady strength
That helms our ships, and something of the Greek,
The cool clear passion of Platonic thought
Behind the fringe of his Olympian beard
And broad Homeric brows, confronting him
Gravely.
        There was a burden of mystery
Brooding on all that night; and, when at last
Chapman replied, I knew he felt it, too.
The curious pedantry of his wonted speech
Was charged with living undertones, like truths
Too strange and too tremendous to be breathed
Save thro' a mask. And though, in lines that flamed
Once with strange rivalry, Shakespeare himself defied
Chapman, that spirit " by spirits taught to write
Above a mortal pitch," Will's nimbler sense
Was quick to breathings from beyond our world
And could not hold them lightly.
                  " Ah, then Kit,"
Said Chapman, " had some prescience of his end,
Like many another dreamer. What strange hints
Of things past, present, and to come, there lie
Sealed in the magic pages of that music
Which, laying strong hold on universal laws,
Ranges beyond these mud-walls of the flesh,
Though dull wits fail to follow. It was this
That made men find an oracle in the books
Of Vergil, and an everlasting fount
Of science in the prophets."
                Once again
That haunted silence filled the shadowy room;

And, far away up Bread Street, we could hear
The crowder, piping of black Wormall still:—

> *" He had a friend, once gay and green,*
> *Who died of want alone,*
> *In whose black fate he might have seen*
> *The warning of his own."*

" Strange he should ask a hod-man like myself
To crown that miracle of his April age,"
Said Chapman, murmuring softly under breath,
" Amorous Leander, beautiful and young . . .
Why, Nash, had I been only charged to raise
Out of its grave in the green Hellespont
The body of that boy,
To make him sparkle and leap thro' the cold waves
And fold young Hero to his heart again,
The task were scarce as hard.

               But . . . stranger still,"—
And his next words, although I hardly knew
All that he meant, went tingling through my flesh —
" Before you spoke, before I knew his wish,
I had begun to write!

            I knew and loved
His work. Himself I hardly knew at all;
And yet — I know him now! I have heard him now
And, since he pledged me in so rare a cup,
I'll lift and drink to him, though lightnings fall
From envious gods to scourge me. I will lift
This cup in darkness to the soul that reigns
In light on Helicon. Who knows how near?

For I have thought, sometimes, when I have tried
To work his will, the hand that moved my pen
Was mine, and yet — not mine. The bodily mask
Is mine, and sometimes, dull as clay, it sleeps
With old Musæus. Then strange flashes come,
Oracular glories, visionary gleams,
And the mask moves, not of itself, and sings."

"I know that thought," said Nash. "A mighty ship,
A lightning-shattered wreck, out in that night,
Unseen, has foundered thundering. We sit here
Snug on the shore, and feel the wash of it,
The widening circles running to our feet.
Can such a soul go down to glut the sharks
Without one ripple? Here comes one sprinkle of spray.
Listen!" And through that night, quick and intense,
And hushed for thunder, tingled once again,
Like a thin wire, the crowder's distant tune:—

> "Had he been prenticed to the trade
> His father followed still,
> This exit he had never made,
> Nor played a part so ill."

"Here is another," said Nash, "I know not why;
But like a weed in the long wash, I too
Was moved, not of myself, to a tune like this.
O, I can play the crowder, fiddle a song
On a dead friend, with any the best of you.
Lie and kick heels in the sun on a dead man's grave
And yet — God knows — it is the best we can;
And better than the world's way, to forget."

So saying, like one that murmurs happy words
To torture his own grief, half in self-scorn,
He breathed a scrap of balladry that raised
The mists a moment from that Paradise,
That primal world of innocence, where Kit
In childhood played, outside his father's shop,
Under the sign of the *Golden Shoe*, as thus:—

   A cobbler lived in Canterbury
— He is dead now, poor soul! —
He sat at his door and stitched in the sun,
Nodding and smiling at everyone;
For St. Hugh makes all good cobblers merry,
And often he sang as the pilgrims passed,
"I can hammer a soldier's boot,
And daintily glove a dainty foot.
Many a sandal from my hand
Has walked the road to Holy Land.
Knights may fight for me, priests may pray for me,
Pilgrims walk the pilgrim's way for me,
I have a work in the world to do!
— *Trowl the bowl, the nut-brown bowl,*
      To good St. Hugh! —
The cobbler must stick to his last."

   And anon he would cry
"Kit! Kit! Kit!" to his little son,
"Look at the pilgrims riding by!
Dance down, hop down, after them, run!"
Then, like an unfledged linnet, out
Would tumble the brave little lad,
With a piping shout,—

" O, look at them, look at them, look at them, Dad!
Priest and prioress, abbot and friar,
Soldier and seaman, knight and squire!
How many countries have they seen?
Is there a king there, is there a queen?
Dad, one day,
Thou and I must ride like this,
All along the Pilgrim's Way,
By Glastonbury and Samarcand,
El Dorado and Cathay,
London and Persepolis,
All the way to Holy Land! "

Then, shaking his head as if he knew,
Under the sign of the *Golden Shoe,*
Touched by the glow of the setting sun,
While the pilgrims passed,
The little cobbler would laugh and say:
" When you are old you will understand
'Tis a very long way
To Samarcand!
Why, largely to exaggerate .
Befits not men of small estate,
But — I should say, yes, I should say,
'Tis a hundred miles from where you stand;
And a hundred more, my little son,
A hundred more, to Holy Land! . . .
I have a work in the world to do
—*Trowl the bowl, the nut-brown bowl,*
      To good St. Hugh! —
The cobbler must stick to his last."

"Which last," said Nash, breaking his rhyme off short,
"The crowder, after his kind, would seem to approve.
Well — all the waves from that great wreck out there
Break, and are lost in one with-drawing sigh:

> The little lad that used to play
> Around the cobbler's door,
> Kit Marlowe, Kit Marlowe,
> We shall not see him more.

But — could I tell you how that galleon sank,
Could I but bring you to that hollow whirl,
The black gulf in mid-ocean, where that wreck
Went thundering down, and round it hell still roars,
That were a tale to snap all fiddle-strings."
"Tell me," said Chapman.
                    "Ah, you wondered why,"
Said Nash, "you wondered why he asked your help
To crown that work of his. Why, Chapman, think,
Think of the cobbler's awl — there's a stout lance
To couch at London, there's a conquering point
To carry in triumph through Persepolis!
I tell you Kit was nothing but a child,
When some rich patron of the *Golden Shoe*
Beheld him riding into Samarcand
Upon a broken chair, the which he said
Was a white steed, splashed with the blood of kings.
    When, on that patron's bounty, he did ride
So far as Cambridge, he was a brave lad,
Untamed, adventurous, but still innocent,
O, innocent as the cobbler's little self!

He brought to London just a bundle and stick,
A slender purse, an Ovid, a few scraps
Of song, and all unshielded, all unarmed
A child's heart, packed with splendid hopes and dreams.
I say a child's heart, Chapman, and that phrase
Crowns, not dis-crowns, his manhood.

                    Well — he turned
An honest penny, taking some small part
In plays at the *Red Bull.* And, all the while,
Beyond the paint and tinsel of the stage,
Beyond the greasy cock-pit with its reek
Of orange-peel and civet, as all of these
Were but the clay churned by the glorious rush
Of his white chariots and his burning steeds,
Nay, as the clay were a shadow, his great dreams,
Like bannered legions on some proud crusade,
Empurpling all the deserts of the world,
Swept on in triumph to the glittering towers
Of his abiding City.

             Then — he met
That damned blood-sucking cockatrice, the pug
Of some fine strutting mummer, one of those plagues
Bred by our stage, a puff-ball on the hill
Of Helicon. As for his wench — she too
Had played so many parts that she forgot
The cue for truth. King Puff had taught her well.
He was the vainer and more foolish thing,
She the more poisonous.

                One dark day, to spite
Archer, her latest paramour, a friend
And apple-squire to Puff she set her eyes

JOHN FLETCHER

On Marlowe . . . feigned a joy in his young art,
Murmured his songs, used all her London tricks
To coney-catch the country green-horn. Man,
Kit never even *saw* her painted face!
He pored on books by candle-light and saw
Everything thro' a mist. O, I could laugh
To think of it, only — his up-turned skull
There, in the dark, now that the flesh drops off,
Has laughed enough, a horrible silent laugh,
To think his Angel of Light was, after all,
Only the red-lipped Angel of the Plague.
He was no better than the rest of us,
No worse. He felt the heat. He felt the cold.
He took her down to Deptford to escape
Contagion, and the crashing of sextons' spades
On dead men's bones in every churchyard round;
The jangling bell and the cry, *Bring out your dead.*
And there she told him of her luckless life,
Wedded, deserted, both against her will,
A luckless Eve that never knew the snake.
True and half-true she mixed in one wild lie,
And then — she caught him by the hand and wept.
No death-cart passed to warn him with its bell.
Her eyes, her perfumed hair, and her red mouth,
Her warm white breast, her civet-scented skin,
Swimming before him, in a piteous mist,
Made the lad drunk, and — she was in his arms;
And all that God had meant to wake one day
Under the Sun of Love, suddenly woke
By candle-light and cried, 'The Sun; The Sun!'
And he believed it, Chapman, he believed it!

He was a cobbler's son, and he believed
In Love! Blind, through that mist, he caught at Love,
The everlasting King of all this world.

Kit was not clever. Clever men — like Pomp —
Might jest. And fools might laugh. But when a man,
Simple as all great elemental things,
Makes his whole heart a sacrificial fire
To one whose love is in her supple skin,
There comes a laughter in which jests break up
Like icebergs in a sea of burning marl.
Then dreamers turn to murderers in an hour.
Then topless towers are burnt, and the Ocean-sea
Tramples the proud fleet, down, into the dark,
And sweeps over it, laughing. Come and see,
The heart now of this darkness — no more waves,
But the black central hollow where that wreck
Went down for ever.
                        How should Piers Penniless
Brand that wild picture on the world's black heart? —
Last night I tried the way of the Florentine,
And bruised myself; but we are friends together
Mourning a dead friend, none will ever know! —
Kit, do you smile at poor Piers Penniless,
Measuring it out? Ah, boy, it is my best!
Since hearts must beat, let it be *terza rima,*
A ladder of rhyme that two sad friends alone
May let down, thus, to the last circle of hell."

So saying, and motionless as a man in trance,
Nash breathed the words that raised the veil anew,

Strange intervolving words which, as he spake them,
Moved like the huge slow whirlpool of that pit
Where the wreck sank, the serpentine slow folds
Of the lewd Kraken that sucked it, shuddering, down: —

This is the Deptford Inn. Climb the dark stair.
  Come, come and see Kit Marlowe lying dead!
See, on the table, by that broken chair,

The little phials of paint — the white and red.
  A cut-lawn kerchief hangs behind the door,
Left by his punk, even as the tapster said.

There is the gold-fringed taffeta gown she wore,
  And, on that wine-stained bed, as is most meet,
He lies alone, never to waken more.

O, still as chiselled marble, the frayed sheet
  Folds the still form on that sepulchral bed,
Hides the dead face, and peaks the rigid feet.

Come, come and see Kit Marlowe lying dead!
  Draw back the sheet, ah, tenderly lay bare
The splendour of that Apollonian head;

The gloriole of his flame-coloured hair;
  The lean athletic body, deftly planned
To carry that swift soul of fire and air;

The long thin flanks, the broad breast, and the grand
  Heroic shoulders! Look, what lost dreams lie
Cold in the fingers of that delicate hand;

And, shut within those lyric lips, what cry
   Of unborn beauty, sunk in utter night,
Lost worlds of song, sealed in an unknown sky,

Never to be brought forth, clothed on with light.
   Was this, then, this the secret of his song?—
Who ever loved that loved not at first sight?

It was not Love, not Love, that wrought this wrong;
   And yet — what evil shadow of this dark town
Could quench a soul so flame-like clean and strong,

Strike the young glory of his manhood down,
   Dead, like a dog, dead in a drunken brawl,
Dead for a phial of paint, a taffeta gown?

What if his blood were hot? High over all
   He heard, as in his song the world still hears,
Those angels on the burning heavenly wall

Who chant the thunder-music of the spheres.
   Yet — through the glory of his own young dream
Here did he meet that face, wet with strange tears,

Andromeda, with piteous face astream,
   Hailing him, Perseus. In her treacherous eyes
As in dark pools the mirrored stars will gleam,

Here did he see his own eternal skies;
   And here — she laughed, nor found the dream amiss;
But bade him pluck and eat — in Paradise.

Here did she hold him, broken up with bliss,
  Here, like a supple snake, around him coiled,
Here did she pluck his heart out with a kiss,

Here were the wings clipped and the glory soiled,
  Here adders coupled in the pure white shrine,
Here was the Wine spilt, and the Shew-bread spoiled.

Black was that feast, though he who poured the Wine
  Dreamed that he poured it in high sacrament.
Deep in her eyes he saw his own eyes shine,

Beheld Love's god-head and was well content.
  Subtly her hand struck the pure silver note,
The throbbing chord of passion that God meant

To swell the bliss of heaven. Round his young throat
  She wound her swarthy tresses; then, with eyes
Half mad to see their power, half mad to gloat,

Half mad to batten on their own devilries,
  And mark what heaven-born splendours they could quell,
She held him quivering in a mesh of lies,

And in soft broken speech began to tell —
  There as, against her heart, throbbing he lay —
The truth that hurled his soul from heaven to hell.

Quivering, she watched the subtle whip-lash flay
  The white flesh of the dreams of his pure youth;
Then sucked the blood and left them cold as clay.

Luxuriously she lashed him with the truth.
   Against his mouth her subtle mouth she set
To show, as through a mask, O, without ruth,

As through a cold clay mask (brackish and wet
   With what strange tears!) it was not his, not his,
The kiss that through his quivering lips she met.

Kissing him, *" Thus,"* she whispered, *" did he kiss.*
   Ah, is the sweetness like a sword, then, sweet?
Last night — ah, kiss again — aching with bliss,

Thus was I made his own, from head to feet."
   — A sudden agony thro' his body swept
Tempestuously.—*" Our wedded pulses beat*

Like this and this; and then, at dawn, he slept."
   She laughed, pouting her lips against his cheek
To drink; and, as in answer, Marlowe wept.

As a dead man in dreams, he heard her speak.
   Clasped in the bitter grave of that sweet clay,
Wedded and one with it, he moaned. Too weak

Even to lift his head, sobbing, he lay.
   Then, slowly, as their breathings rose and fell,
He felt the storm of passion, far away,

Gather. The shuddering waves began to swell.
   And, through the menace of the thunder-roll,
The thin quick lightnings, thrilling through his hell,

Lightnings that hell itself could not control
  (Even while she strove to bow his neck anew)
Woke the great slumbering legions of his soul.

Sharp was that severance of the false and true,
  Sharp as a sword drawn from a shuddering wound.
But they, that were one flesh, were cloven in two.

Flesh leapt from clasping flesh, without a sound.
  He plucked his body from her white embrace,
And cast him down, and grovelled on the ground.

Yet, ere he went, he strove once more to trace,
  Deep in her eyes, the loveliness he knew;
Then — spat his hatred into her smiling face.

She clung to him. He flung her off. He drew
  His dagger, thumbed the blade, and laughed —" Poor
    punk!
What? Would you make me your own murderer, too?"

  .   .   .   .

" That was the day of our great feast," said Nash,
" Aboard the *Golden Hind*. The grand old hulk
Was drawn up for the citizens' wonderment
At Deptford. Ay, Piers Penniless was there!
Soaked and besotted as I was, I saw
Everything. On her poop the minstrels played,
And round her sea-worn keel, like meadow-sweet
Curtseying round a lightning-blackened oak,

Prentices and their sweethearts, heel and toe,
Danced the brave English dances, clean and fresh
As May.
    But in her broad gun-guarded waist
Once red with British blood, long tables groaned
For revellers not so worthy. Where her guns
Had raked the seas, barrels of ale were sprung,
Bestrid by roaring tipplers. Where at night
The storm-beat crew silently bowed their heads
With Drake before the King of Life and Death,
A strumpet wrestled with a mountebank
For pence, a loose-limbed Lais with a clown
Of Cherry Hilton. Leering at their lewd twists,
Cross-legged upon the deck, sluggish with sack,
Like a squat toad sat Puff . . .
Propped up against the bulwarks, at his side,
Archer, his apple-squire, hiccoughed a bawdy song.

Suddenly, through that orgy, with wild eyes,
Yet with her customary smile, O, there
I saw in day-light what Kit Marlowe saw
Through blinding mists, the face of his first love.
She stood before her paramour on the deck,
Cocking her painted head to right and left,
Her white teeth smiling, but her voice a hiss:
' Quickly,' she said to Archer, ' come away,
Of there'll be blood spilt!'
      ' Better blood than wine,'
Said Archer, struggling to his feet, ' but who,
Who would spill blood?'
      ' Marlowe!' she said.

Then Puff
Reeled to his feet. 'What, Kit, the cobbler's son?
The lad that broke his leg at the *Red Bull,*
Tamburlaine-Marlowe, he that would chain kings
To's chariot-wheel? What, is he rushing hither?
He would spill blood for Gloriana, hey?
O, my Belphœbe, you will crack my sides?
Was this the wench that shipped a thousand squires?
O, ho! But here he comes. Now, solemnly, lads,—
Now walk the angels on the walls of heaven
To entertain divine Zenocrate!'

And there stood Kit, high on the storm-scarred poop,
Against the sky, bare-headed. I saw his face,
Pale, innocent, just the clear face of that boy
Who walked to Cambridge with a bundle and stick,—
The little cobbler's son. Yet — there I caught
My only glimpse of how the sun-god looked,
And only for one moment.
                              When he saw
His mistress, his face whitened, and he shook.
Down to the deck he came, a poor weak man;
And yet — by God — the only man that day
In all our drunken crew.
                         'Come along, Kit,'
Cried Puff, 'we'll all be friends now, all take hands,
And dance — ha! ha!— the shaking of the sheets!'
Then Archer, shuffling a step, raised his cracked voice
In Kit's own song to a falsetto tune,
Snapping one hand, thus over his head as he danced:—

> *' Come, live with me, and be my love,*
> *And we will all the pleasures prove!'* . . .

Puff reeled between, laughing. 'Damn you,' cried Kit,
And, catching the fat swine by his round soft throat,
Hurled him headlong, crashing across the tables,
To lie and groan in the red bilge of wine
That washed the scuppers.

                Kit gave him not one glance.
'Archer,' he said in a whisper.

                      Instantly
A long thin rapier flashed in Archer's hand.
The ship was one wild uproar. Women screamed
And huddled together. A drunken clamorous ring
Seethed around Marlowe and his enemy.
Kit drew his dagger, slowly, and I knew
Blood would be spilt.

               'Here, take my rapier, Kit!'
I cried across the crowd, seeing the lad
Was armed so slightly. But he did not hear.
I could not reach him.

             All at once he leapt
Like a wounded tiger, past the rapier point
Straight at his enemy's throat. I saw his hand
Up-raised to strike! I heard a harlot's scream,
And, in mid-air, the hand stayed, quivering, white,
A frozen menace.

           I saw a yellow claw
Twisting the dagger out of that frozen hand;
I saw his own steel in that yellow grip,
His own lost lightning raised to strike at him!

I saw it flash! I heard the driving grunt
Of him that struck! Then, with a shout, the crowd
Sundered, and through the gap, a blank red thing
Streaming with blood, came the blind face of Kit,
Reeling, to me! And I, poor drunken I,
Held my arms wide for him. Here, on my breast,
With one great sob, he burst his heart and died."

   .   .   .   .   .

Nash ceased. And, far away down Friday Street,
The crowder with his fiddle wailed again:

> *"Blaspheming Tambolin must die*
> *And Faustus meet his end.*
> *Repent, repent, or presentlie*
> *To hell ye must descend."*

And, as in answer, Chapman slowly breathed
Those mightiest lines of Marlowe's own despair:

> *"Think'st thou that I who saw the face of God,*
> *And tasted the eternal joys of heaven,*
> *Am not tormented with ten thousand hells?"*

"Ah, you have said it," said Nash, "and there you know
Why Kit desired your hand to crown his work.
He reverenced you as one whose temperate eyes
Austere and grave, could look him through and through;
One whose firm hand could grasp the reins of law
And guide those furious horses of the sun,
As Ben and Will can guide them, where you will.
His were, perchance, the noblest steeds of all,
And from their nostrils blew a fierier dawn

Above the world.   That glory is his own;
But where he fell, he fell.   Before his hand
Had learned to quell them, he was dashed to the earth.
'Tis yours to show that good men honoured him.
For, mark this, Chapman, since Kit Marlowe fell,
There will be fools that, in the name of Art,
Will wallow in the mire, crying 'I fall,
I fall from heaven!'— fools that have only heard
From earth, the rumour of those golden hooves
Far, far above them.   Yes, you know the kind,
The fools that scorn Will for his lack of fire
Because he quells the storms they never knew,
And rides above the thunder; fools of Art
That skip and vex, like little vicious fleas,
Their only Helicon, some green madam's breast.
Art!   Art!   O, God, that I could send my soul,
In one last wave, from that night-hidden wreck,
Across the shores of all the years to be;
O, God, that like a crowder I might shake
Their blind dark casements with the pity of it,
Piers Penniless his ballad, a poor scrap,
That but for lack of time, and hope and pence,
He might have bettered!   For a dead man's sake,
Thus would the wave break, thus the crowder cry:—

           Dead, like a dog upon the road;
               Dead, for a harlot's kiss;
           The Apollonian throat and brow,
           The lyric lips, so silent now,
           The flaming wings that heaven bestowed
               For loftier airs than this!

[94]

The sun-like eyes whose light and life
    Had gazed an angel's down,
That burning heart of honey and fire,
Quenched and dead for an apple-squire,
Quenched at the thrust of a mummer's knife,
    Dead — for a taffeta gown!

The wine that God had set apart,
    The noblest wine of all,
Wine of the grapes that angels trod,
The vintage of the glory of God,
The crimson wine of that rich heart,
    Spilt in a drunken brawl,

Poured out to make a steaming bath
    That night in the Devil's Inn,
A steaming bath of living wine
Poured out for Circe and her swine,
A bath of blood for a harlot
    To supple and sleek her skin.

And many a fool that finds it sweet
    Through all the years to be,
Crowning a lie with Marlowe's fame,
Will ape the sin, will ape the shame,
Will ape our captain in defeat;
    But — not in victory;

Till Art become a leaping-house,
    And Death be crowned as Life,
And one wild jest out-shine the soul

Of Truth . . . O, fool, is this your goal?
You are not our Kit Marlowe,
   But the drunkard with the knife;

Not Marlowe, but the Jack-o'-Lent
   That lured him o'er the fen!
O, ay, the tavern is in its place,
And the punk's painted smiling face,
But where is our Kit Marlowe
   The man, the king of men?

Passion? You kiss the painted mouth,
   The hand that clipped his wings,
The hand that into his heart she thrust
And tuned him to her whimpering lust,
And played upon his quivering youth
   As a crowder plucks the strings.

But he who dared the thunder-roll,
   Whose eagle-wings could soar,
Buffeting down the clouds of night,
To beat against the Light of Light,
That great God-blinded eagle-soul,
   We shall not see him more."

V

THE COMPANION OF A MILE

V

THE COMPANION OF A MILE

THWACK! *Thwack!* One early dawn upon our door
   I heard the bladder of some motley fool
Bouncing, and all the dusk of London shook
With bells! I leapt from bed,— had I forgotten?—
I flung my casement wide and craned my neck
Over the painted Mermaid. There he stood,
His right leg yellow and his left leg blue,
With jingling cap, a sheep-bell at his tail,
Wielding his eel-skin bladder,— *bang! thwack! bang!*—
Catching a comrade's head with the recoil
And skipping away! All Bread Street dimly burned
Like a reflected sky, green, red and white
With littered branches, ferns and hawthorn-clouds;
For, round Sir Fool, a frolic morrice-troop
Of players, poets, prentices, mad-cap queans,
Robins and Marians, coloured like the dawn,
And sparkling like the green-wood whence they came
With their fresh boughs all dewy from the dark,
Clamoured, *Come down! Come down, and let us in!*
High over these, I suddenly saw Sir Fool
Leap to a sign-board, swing to a conduit-head,
And perch there, gorgeous on the morning sky,
Tossing his crimson cocks-comb to the blue
And crowing like Chanticleer, *Give them a rouse!*

Tickle it, tabourer!   Nimbly, lasses, nimbly!
Tuck up your russet petticoats and dance!
Let the Cheape know it is the first of May!

And as I seized shirt, doublet and trunk-hose,
I saw the hobby-horse come cantering down,
A paste-board steed, dappled a rosy white
Like peach-bloom, bridled with purple, bitted with gold,
A crimson foot-cloth on his royal flanks,
And, riding him, His Majesty of the May!
Round him the whole crowd frolicked with a shout,
And as I stumbled down the crooked stair
I heard them break into a dance and sing:—

SONG

I

Into the woods we'll trip and go,
Up and down and to and fro,
Under the moon to fetch in May,
And two by two till break of day,
        A-maying,
        A-playing,
For Love knows no gain-saying!
Wisdom trips not?   Even so —
Come, young lovers, trip and go,
        Trip and go.

II

Out of the woods we'll dance and sing
Under the morning-star of Spring,
Into the town with our fresh boughs

And knock at every sleeping house,
    Not sighing,
    Or crying,
Though Love knows no denying!
Then, round your summer queen and king,
Come, young lovers, dance and sing,
    Dance and sing!

"*Chorus,*" the great Fool tossed his gorgeous crest,
And lustily crew against the deepening dawn,
"*Chorus,*" till all the Cheape caught the refrain,
And, with a double thunder of frolic feet,
Its ancient nut-brown tabors woke the Strand:—

    A-maying,
    A-playing,
For Love knows no gain-saying!
Wisdom trips not? Even so,—
Come, young lovers, trip and go,
    Trip and go.

Into the Mermaid with a shout they rushed
As I shot back the bolts, and *bang, thwack, bang,*
The bladder bounced about me. What cared I?
This was all England's holy-day! "Come in,
My yellow-hammers," roared the Friar Tuck
Of this mad morrice, "come you into church,
My nightingales, my scraps of Lincoln green,
And hear my sermon!" On a window-seat
He stood, against the diamonded rich panes
In the old oak parlour and, throwing back his hood,

Who should it be but Ben, rare Ben himself?
The wild troop laughed around him, some a-sprawl
On tables, kicking parti-coloured heels,
Some with their Marians jigging on their knees,
And, in the front of all, the motley fool
Cross-legged upon the rushes.

              O, I knew him,—
Will Kemp, the player, who danced from London town
To Norwich in nine days and was proclaimed
Freeman of Marchaunt Venturers and hedge-king
Of English morrice-dancery for ever!
His nine-days' wonder, through the country-side
Was hawked by every ballad-monger. Kemp
Raged at their shake-rag Muses. None but I
Guessed ever for what reason, since he chose
His anticks for himself and, in his games,
Was more than most May-fools fantastical.
I watched his thin face, as he rocked and crooned,
Shaking the squirrels' tails around his ears;
And, out of all the players I had seen,
His face was quickest through its clay to flash
The passing mood. Though not a muscle stirred,
The very skin of it seemed to flicker and gleam
With little summer lightnings of the soul
At every fleeting fancy. For a man
So quick to bleed at a pin-prick or to leap
Laughing through hell to save a butterfly,
This world was difficult; and perchance he found
In his fantastic games that open road
Which even Will Shakespeare only found at last
In motley and with some wild straws in his hair.

But "Drawer! drawer!" bellowed Friar Ben,
"Make ready a righteous breakfast while I preach;—
Tankards of nut-brown ale, and cold roast beef,
Cracknels, old cheese, flaunes, tarts and clotted cream,
Hath any a wish not circumscribed by these?"

"A white-pot custard, for my white-pot queen,"
Cried Kemp, waving his bauble, "mark this, boy,
A white-pot custard for my queen of May,—
She is not here, but that concerns not thee!—
A white-pot Mermaid custard, with a crust,
Lashings of cream, eggs, apple-pulse and spice,
A little sugar and manchet bread. Away!
Be swift!"

        And as I bustled to and fro,
The Friar raised his big brown fists again
And preached in mockery of the Puritans
Who thought to strip the moonshine wings from Mab,
Tear down the May-poles, rout our English games,
And drive all beauty back into the sea.

Then laughter and chatter and clashing tankards drowned
All but their May-day jollity a-while.
But, as their breakfast ended, and I sank
Gasping upon a bench, there came still more
Poets and players crowding into the room;
And one — I only knew him as Sir John —
Waved a great ballad at Will Kemp and laughed,
"Atonement, Will, atonement!"

               "What," groaned Kemp,
"Another penny poet? How many lies

Does *this* rogue tell?   Sir, I have suffered much
From these Melpomenes and strawberry quills,
And think them better at their bloody lines
On *The Blue Lady*.   Sir, they set to work
At seven o'clock in the morning, the same hour
That I, myself, that's *Cavaliero* Kemp,
With heels of feather and heart of cork, began
Frolickly footing, from the great Lord Mayor
Of London, tow'rds the worshipful Master Mayor
Of Norwich."

        " Nay, Kemp, this is a May-day tune,
A morrice of country rhymes, made by a poet
Who thought it shame so worthy an act as thine
Should wither in oblivion if the Muse
With her Castalian showers could keep it green.
And while the fool nid-nodded all in time,
Sir John, in swinging measure, trolled this tale:—

I

With Georgie Sprat, my overseer, and Thomas Slye, my
      tabourer,
    And William Bee, my courier, when dawn emblazed the
      skies,
I met a tall young butcher as I danced by little Sudbury,
    Head-master o' morrice-dancers all, high headborough of
      hyes.

By Sudbury, by Sudbury, by little red-roofed Sudbury,
    He wished to dance a mile with me!   I made a courtly
      bow:

I fitted him with morrice-bells, with treble, bass and tenor
    bells,
  And *" Tickle your tabor, Tom,"* I cried, *" we're going to
    market now."*

And rollicking down the lanes we dashed, and frolicking up
    the hills we clashed,
  And like a sail behind me flapped his great white frock
    a-while,
Till, with a gasp, he sank and swore that he could dance
    with me no more;
  And — over the hedge a milk-maid laughed, *Not dance
    with him a mile?*

" You lout!" she laughed, " I'll leave my pail, and dance
    with him for cakes and ale!
  I'll dance a mile for love," she laughed, " and win my
    wager, too.
Your feet are shod and mine are bare; but when could
    leather dance on air?
  A milk-maid's feet can fall as fair and light as falling
    dew."

I fitted her with morrice-bells, with treble, bass and tenor
    bells:
  The fore-bells, as I linked them at her throat, how soft
    they sang!
Green linnets in a golden nest, they chirped and trembled
    on her breast,
  And, faint as elfin blue-bells, at her nut-brown ankles
    rang.

I fitted her with morrice-bells that sweetened into wood-
    bine bells,
  And trembled as I hung them there and crowned her
    sunny brow:
"Strike up," she laughed, "my summer king!" And all
    her bells began to ring,
  And *"Tickle your tabor, Tom,"* I cried, *"we're going to
    Sherwood now!"*

When cocks were crowing, and light was growing, and
    horns were blowing, and milk-pails flowing,
  We swam thro' waves of emerald gloom along a chestnut
    aisle,
Then, up a shining hawthorn-lane, we sailed into the sun
    again,
  Will Kemp and his companion, his companion of a mile.

"Truer than most," snarled Kemp, "but mostly lies!
And why does he forget the miry lanes
By Brainford with thick woods on either side,
And the deep holes, where I could find no ease
But skipped up to my waist?" A crackling laugh
Broke from his lips which, if he had not worn
The cap and bells, would scarce have roused the mirth
Of good Sir John, who roundly echoed it,
Then waved his hand and said, "Nay, but he treats
Your morrice in the spirit of Lucian, Will,
Who thought that dancing was no mushroom growth,
But sprung from the beginning of the world
When Love persuaded earth, air, water, fire,
And all the jarring elements to move

[106]

In measure. Right to the heart of it, my lad,
The song goes, though the skin mislike you so."
"Nay, an there's more of it, I'll sing it, too!
'Tis a fine tale, Sir John, I have it by heart,
Although 'tis lies throughout." Up leapt Will Kemp,
And crouched and swayed, and swung his bauble round,
Marking the measure as they trolled the tale,
Chanting alternately, each answering each.

II

The Fool

The tabor fainted far away behind us, but her feet that day
 They beat a rosier morrice o'er the fairy-circled green.

Sir John

And o'er a field of buttercups, a field of lambs and buttercups,
 We danced along a cloth of gold, a summer king and
  queen!

The Fool

And straying we went, and swaying we went, with lamb-
 kins round us playing we went;
 Her face uplift to drink the sun, and not for me her smile,
We danced, a king and queen of May, upon a fleeting holy-
 day,
 But O, she'd won her wager, my companion of a mile!

Sir John

Her rosy lips they never spoke, though every rosy foot-fall
 broke

[107]

The dust, the dust to Eden-bloom; and, past the throbbing blue,
All ordered to her rhythmic feet, the stars were dancing with
my sweet,
And all the world a morrice-dance!

The Fool

She knew not; but I knew!
Love like Amphion with his lyre, made all the elements con-
spire
To build His world of music. All in rhythmic rank and
file,
I saw them in their cosmic dance, catch hands across, re-
tire, advance,
For me and my companion, my companion of a mile!

Sir John

The little leaves on every tree, the rivers winding to the
sea,
The swinging tides, the wheeling winds, the rolling
heavens above,
Around the May-pole Igdrasil, they worked the Morrice-
master's will,
Persuaded into measure by the all-creative Love.

That hour I saw, from depth to height, this wildering universe unite!
The lambs of God around us and His passion in every
flower!

The Fool

His grandeur in the dust, His dust a blaze of blinding
    majesty,
  And all His immortality in one poor mortal hour.

And Death was but a change of key in Life the golden
    melody,
  And Time became Eternity, and Heaven a fleeting smile;
For all was each and each was all, and all a wedded unity,
  Her heart in mine, and mine in my companion of a mile.

Thwack! Thwack! He whirled his bauble round about,
"This fellow beats them all," he cried, "the worst
Those others wrote was that I hopped from York
To Paris with a mortar on my head.
This fellow sends me leaping through the clouds
To buss the moon! The best is yet to come;
Strike up, Sir John! Ha! ha! You know no more?"
Kempt leapt upon a table. "Clear the way,"
He cried, and with a great stamp of his foot
And a wild crackling laugh, drew all to hark.
  "With hey and ho, through thick and thin,
    The hobby-horse is forgotten.
  But I must finish what I begin,
    Tho' all the roads be rotten.
"By all those twenty thousand chariots, Ben,
Hear this true tale they shall! Now, let me see,
Where was Will Kemp? Bussing the moon's pale mouth?
Ah, yes!" He crouched above the listening throng,—
"*Good as a play*," I heard one whispering quean,—

[109]

And, waving his bauble, shuffling with his feet
In a dance that marked the time, he sank his voice
As if to breathe great secrets, and so sang:—

III

At Melford town, at Melford town, at little grey-roofed
    Melford town,
  A long mile from Sudbury, upon the village green,
We danced into a merry rout of country-folk that skipt
    about
  A hobby-horse, a May-pole, and a laughing white-pot
    queen.

They thronged about us as we stayed, and there I gave my
    sunshine maid
  An English crown for cakes and ale — her dancing was
    so true!
And "Nay," she said, "I danced my mile for love!" I
    answered with a smile,
  "'Tis but a silver token, lass, thou'st won that wager,
    too."

I took my leash of morrice-bells, my treble, bass and tenor
    bells,
  They pealed like distant marriage-bells! And up came
    William Bee
With Georgie Sprat, my overseer, and Thomas Slye, my
    tabourer,
  "Farewell," she laughed, and vanished with a Suffolk
    courtesie.

I leapt away to Rockland, and from Rockland on to Hingham,
 From Hingham on to Norwich, sirs! I hardly heard
  a-while
The throngs that followed after, with their shouting and
 their laughter,
 For a shadow danced beside me, my companion of a mile!

At Norwich, by St. Giles his gate, I entered, and the Mayor
 in state,
 With all the rosy knights and squires for twenty miles
  about,
With trumpets and with minstrelsy, was waiting there to
 welcome me;
 And, as I skipt into the street, the City raised a shout.

They gave me what I did not seek! I fed on roasted swans
 a week!
 They pledged me in their malmsey, and they lined me
  warm with ale!
They sleeked my skin with red-deer pies, and all that runs
 and swims and flies;
 But, through the clashing wine-cups, O, I heard her
  clanking pail.

And, rising from his crimson chair, the worshipful and
 portly Mayor
 Bequeathed me forty shillings every year that I should
  live,
With five good angels in my hand that I might drink while
 I could stand!

They gave me golden angels! What I lacked they could
    not give.

They made Will Kemp, thenceforward, sirs, Freeman of
    Marchaunt Venturers!
They hoped that I would dance again from Norwich up
    to York;
Then they asked me, all together, had I met with right May
    weather,
    And they praised my heels of feather, and my heart, my
    heart of cork.

.   .   .   .

As I came home by Sudbury, by little red-roofed Sudbury,
    I waited for my bare-foot maid, among her satin kine!
I heard a peal of wedding-bells, of treble, bass and tenor
    bells:
    "Ring well," I cried, "this bridal morn! You soon
    shall ring for mine!"

I found her foot-prints in the grass, just where she stood
    and saw me pass,
    I stood within her own sweet field and waited for my
    may.
I laughed. The dance has turned about! I stand within:
    she'll pass without,
    And — *down the road the wedding came, the road I
    danced that day!*

*I saw the wedding-folk go by, with laughter and with
    minstrelsy,
    I gazed across her own sweet hedge, I caught her happy
    smile,*

I saw the tall young butcher pass to little red-roofed Sud-
  bury,
  His bride upon his arm, my lost companion of a mile.

Down from his table leapt the motley Fool.
His bladder bounced from head to ducking head,
His crackling laugh rang high,—" Sir John, I danced
In February, and the song says May!
A fig for all your poets, liars all!
Away to Fenchurch Street, lasses and lads,
They hold high revel there this May-day morn.
Away!" The mad-cap throng echoed the cry.
He drove them with his bauble through the door;
Then, as the last gay kerchief fluttered out
He gave one little sharp sad lingering cry
As of a lute-string breaking. He turned back
And threw himself along a low dark bench;
His jingling cap was crumpled in his fist,
And, as he lay there, all along Cheapside
The happy voices of his comrades rang:—

  Out of the woods we'll dance and sing
  Under the morning-star of Spring,
  Into the town with our fresh boughs
  And knock at every sleeping house,
      Not sighing,
      Or crying,
  Though Love knows no denying!
  Then, round your summer queen and king,
  Come, young lovers, dance and sing,
      Dance and sing!

[113]

His motley shoulders heaved. I touched his arm,
"What ails you, sir?" He raised his thin white face,
Wet with the May-dew still. A few stray petals
Clung in his tangled hair. He leapt to his feet,
"'Twas February, but I danced, boy, danced
In May! Can you do this?" Forward he bent
Over his feet, and shuffled it, heel and toe,
Out of the Mermaid, singing his old song —
    A-maying,
    A-playing,
   For Love knows no gain-saying!
  Wisdom trips not? Even so,—
  Come, young lovers, trip and go,
    Trip and go.

Five minutes later, over the roaring Strand,
Chorus, I heard him crow, and half the town
Reeled into music under his crimson comb.

VI

BIG BEN

VI

BIG BEN

GODS, what a hubbub shook our cobwebs out
        The day that Chapman, Marston and our Ben
Waited in Newgate for the hangman's hands.
Chapman and Marston had been prisoned first
For some imagined insult to the Scots
In *Eastward Ho,* the play they wrote with Ben.
But Ben was famous now, and our brave law
Would fain have winked and passed the big man by.
The lesser men had straightway been condemned
To have their ears cut off, their noses slit,
With other tortures.

                    Ben had risen at that!
He gripped his cudgel, called for a quart of ale,
Then like Helvellyn with his rocky face
And mountain-belly, he surged along Cheapside,
Snorting with wrath, and rolled into the gaol,
To share the punishment.

                    "There is my mark!
'Tis not the first time you have branded me,"
Said our big Ben, and thrust his broad left thumb
Branded with T for Tyburn, into the face
Of every protest. "That's the mark you gave me
Because I killed my man in Spitalfields,
A duel honest as any your courtiers fight.

[117]

But I was no Fitzdotterel, bore no gules
And azure, robbed no silk-worms for my hose,
I was Ben Jonson, out of Annandale,
Bricklayer in common to the good Lord God.
You branded me. I wear no three-piled ruff.
You cannot rub it out."
                    The Mermaid Inn
Buzzed like a hornet's nest, upon the day
Fixed for their mutilation. And the stings
Were ready, too; for rapiers flashed and clashed
Among the tankards. Dekker was there, and Nash,
Brome (Jonson's body-servant, whom he taught
His art of verse and, more than that, to love him,)
And half a dozen more. They planned to meet
The prisoners going to Tyburn, and attempt
A desperate rescue.
                    All at once we heard
A great gay song come marching down the street,
A single voice, and twenty marching men,
Then the full chorus, twenty voices strong:—

> The prentice whistles at break of day
>   All under fair roofs and towers,
> When the old Cheap openeth every way
>   Her little sweet inns like flowers;
> And he sings like a lark, both early and late,
>   To think, if his house take fire,
> At the good *Green Dragon* in Bishopsgate
>   He may drink to his heart's desire.

Chorus: Or sit at his ease in the old *Cross Keys*
            And drink to his heart's desire.

But I, as I walk by *Red Rose Lane,*
   Tho' it warmeth my heart to see
The Swan, The Golden Hind, and *The Crane,*
   With the door set wide for me;
Tho' Signs like daffodils paint the strand
   When the thirsty bees begin,
Of all the good taverns in Engeland
   My choice is — *The Mermaid Inn.*

Chorus: There is much to be said for *The Saracen's Head,*
        But my choice is *The Mermaid Inn.*

Into the tavern they rushed, these roaring boys.
"Now broach your ripest and your best," they cried.
  "All's well! They are all released! They are on the
    way!
Old Camden and young Selden worked the trick.
Where is Dame Dimpling? Where's our jolly hostess?
Tell her the Mermaid Tavern will have guests:
We are sent to warn her. She must raid Cook's Row,
And make their ovens roar. Nobody dines
This day with old Duke Humphrey. Red-deer pies,
Castles of almond crust, a shield of brawn
Big as the nether mill-stone, barrels of wine,
Three roasted peacocks! Ben is on the way!"
Then all the rafters rang with song again:—

    There was a Prince — long since, long since?—
      To East-Cheape did resort,
    For that he loved *The Blue Boar's Head*
      Far better than Crown or Court;

[119]

But old King Harry in Westminster
    Hung up, for all to see,
Three bells of power in St. Stephen's Tower,
    Yea, bells of a thousand and three.

Chorus: Three bells of power in a timber tower,
      Thirty thousand and three.

For Harry the Fourth was a godly king
    And loved great godly bells!
He bade them ring and he bade them swing
    Till a man might hear nought else.
In every tavern it soured the sack
    With discord and with din;
But they drowned it all in a madrigal
    Like this, at the *Mermaid Inn.*

Chorus: They drowned it all in a madrigal
      Like this, at the *Mermaid Inn.*

"But how did Selden work it?"—"Nobody knows.
They will be here anon. Better ask Will.
He's the magician!"—"Ah, here comes Dame Dimpling!"
And, into the rollicking chaos our good Dame
— A Dame of only two and thirty springs —
All lavender and roses and white kerchief,
Bustled, to lay the tables.
                Fletcher flung
His arm around her waist and kissed her cheek.
But all she said was *" One — two — three — four — five —
Six at a pinch, in yonder window-seat."*

[120]

" A health to our Dame Dimpling," Beaumont cried,
And Dekker, leaping on the old black settle,
Led all their tumult into a song again:—

What is the Mermaid's merriest toast?
  Our hostess — good Dame Dimpling!
Who is it rules the Mermaid roast?
Who is it bangs the Mermaid host,
Tho' her hands be soft as her heart almost?
      Dame Dimpling!

She stands at the board in her fresh blue gown
  With the sleeves tucked up — Dame Dimpling!
She rolls the white dough up and down
And her pies are crisp, and her eyes are brown.
So — she is the Queen of all this town,—
      Dame Dimpling!

Her sheets are white as black-thorn bloom,
  White as her neck, Dame Dimpling!
Her lavender sprigs in the London gloom
Make every little bridal-room
A country nook of fresh perfume,—
      Dame Dimpling!

She wears white lace on her dark brown hair:
  And a rose on her breast, Dame Dimpling!
And who can show you a foot as fair
Or an ankle as neat when she climbs the stair,
Taper in hand, and head in the air,
And a rose in her cheek? — O, past compare,
      Dame Dimpling!

"But don't forget those oyster-pies," cried Lyly,
"Nor the roast beef," roared Dekker. "Prove yourself
The Muse of meat and drink."

                 There was a shout
In Bread Street, and our windows all swung wide,
Six heads at each.

                 Nat Field bestrode our sign
And kissed the painted Mermaid on her lips,
Then waved his tankard.

                 "Here they come," he cried.
"Camden and Selden, Chapman and Marston, too,
And half Will's company with our big Ben
Riding upon their shoulders."

                 "Look!" cried Dekker,
"But where is Atlas now? O, let them have it!
A thumping chorus, lads! Let the roof crack!"
And all the Mermaid clashed and banged again
In thunderous measure to the marching tune
That rolled down Bread Street, forty voices strong:—

    At *Ypres Inn,* by *Wring-wren lane,*
      Old John of Gaunt would dine:
    He scarce had opened an oyster or twain,
      Or drunk one flagon of wine,
    When, all along the Vintry Ward,
      He heard the trumpets blow,
    And a voice that roared —"If thou love thy lord,
      Tell John of Gaunt to go!"

Chorus: A great voice roared —"If thou love thy lord,
          Tell John of Gaunt to go!"

Then into the room rushed Haviland
    That fair fat Flemish host,
"They are marching hither with sword and brand,
    Ten thousand men — almost!
It is these oysters or thy sweet life,
    Thy blood or the best of the bin! —"
"Proud Pump, avaunt!" quoth John of Gaunt,
    "I will dine at the *Mermaid Inn!*"

Chorus: "Proud Pump, avaunt!" quoth John of Gaunt,
      "There is wine at the *Mermaid Inn!*"

And in came Ben like a great galleon poised
High on the white crest of a shouting wave,
And then the feast began. The fragrant steam
As from the kitchens of Olympus drew
A throng of ragged urchins to our doors.
Ben ordered them a castellated pie
That rolled a cloud around them where they sat
Munching upon the cobble stones. Our casements
Dripped with the golden dews of Helicon;
And, under the warm feast our cellarage
Gurgled and foamed in the delicious cool
With crimson freshets —

           "Tell us," cried Nat Field,
When pipes began to puff. "How did you work it?"
Camden chuckled and tugged his long white beard.
"Out of the mouth of babes," he said and shook
His head at Selden! "O, young man, young man,
There's a career before you! Selden did it.

Take my advice, my children. Make young Selden
Solicitor-general to the Mermaid Inn.
That rosy silken smile of his conceals
A scholar! Yes, that suckling lawyer there
Puts my grey beard to shame. His courteous airs
And silken manners hide the nimblest wit
That ever trimmed a sail to catch the wind
Of courtly favour. Mark my words now, Ben,
That youth will sail right up against the wind
By skilful tacking. But you run it fine,
Selden, you run it fine. Take my advice
And don't be too ironical, my boy,
Or even the King will see it."

                                        He chuckled again.
" But tell them of your tractate ! "

                                        " Here it is,"
Quoth Selden, twisting a lighted paper spill,
Then, with his round cherubic face aglow
Lit his long silver pipe,

                                " Why, first," he said,
" Camden being Clarencieux King-at-arms,
He read the King this little tract I wrote
Against tobacco." And the Mermaid roared
With laughter. " Well, you went the way to hang
All three of them," cried Lyly, " and, as for Ben,
His Trinidado goes to bed with him."
" Green gosling, quack no more," Selden replied,
Smiling that rosy silken smile anew.
" The King's a *critic!* When have critics known
The poet from his creatures, God from me?
How many cite Polonius to their sons

JOHN SELDEN

From a Painting Attributed to Sir Peter Lely, in the Bodleian Library, Oxford

And call it Shakespeare? Well, I took my text
From sundry creatures of our great big Ben,
And called it ' Jonson.'

              Camden read it out
Without the flicker of an eye. His beard
Saved us, I think. The King admired his text.
' There is a man,' he read, *' lies at death's door
Thro' taking of tobacco. Yesterday
He voided a bushel of soot.'*

                  ' God bless my soul,
A bushel of soot! think of it!' said the King.
' The man who wrote those great and splendid words,'
Camden replied,— I had prepared his case
Carefully — 'lies in Newgate prison, sire.
His nose and ears await the hangman's knife.'

' Ah,' said the shrewd King, goggling his great eyes
Cannily. ' Did he not defame the Scots?'
' That's true,' said Camden, like a man that hears
Truth for the first time. ' O ay, he defamed 'em '
The King said, very wisely, once again.
' Ah, but,' says Camden, like a man that strives
With more than mortal wit, ' only such Scots
As flout your majesty, and take tobacco.
He is a Scot, himself, and hath the gift
Of preaching.' Then we gave him Jonson's lines
Against Virginia. *' Neither do thou lust
After that tawny weed; for who can tell,
Before the gathering and the making up,
What alligarta may have spawned thereon,'*
Or words to that effect.

[125]

       ' Magneeficent! '
Spluttered the King —' who knows? Who knows, indeed?
That's a grand touch, that Alligarta, Camden! '
' The Scot who wrote those great and splendid words,'
Said Camden, ' languishes in Newgate, sire.
His ears and nose —'
      And there, as we arranged
With Inigo Jones, the ladies of the court
Assailed the King in tears.   Their masque and ball
Would all be ruined.   All their Grecian robes,
Procured at vast expense, were wasted now.
The masque was not half-written.   Master Jones
Had lost his poets.   They were all in gaol.
Their noses and their ears . . . .
       ' God bless my soul,'
Spluttered the King, goggling his eyes again,
' What d'you make of it, Camden? '—
        ' I should say

A Puritan plot, sire; for these justices —
Who love tobacco — use their law, it seems,
To flout your Majesty at every turn.
If this continue, sire, there'll not be left
A loyal ear or nose in all your realm.'
At that, our noble monarch well-nigh swooned.
He hunched his body, padded as it was
Against the assassin's knife, six inches deep
With great green quilts, wagged his enormous head,
Then, in a dozen words, he wooed destruction:
' It is presumption and a high contempt
In subjects to dispute what kings can do,'
He whimpered.   ' Even as it is blasphemy

[126]

To thwart the will of God.'

                                He waved his hand,
And rose. 'These men must be released, at once!'
Then, as I think, to seek a safer place,
He waddled from the room, his rickety legs
Doubling beneath that great green feather-bed
He calls his 'person.'— I shall dream to-night
Of spiders, Camden.— But in half an hour,
Inigo Jones was armed with Right Divine
To save such ears and noses as the ball
Required for its perfection. Think of that!
And let this earthly ball remember, too,
That Chapman, Marston, and our great big Ben
Owe their poor adjuncts to — ten Grecian robes
And 'Jonson' on tobacco! England loves
Her poets, O supremely, when they're dead."
"Selden, you saved *us* in the nick of time;
But Ben has narrowly escaped her love,"
Said Chapman gravely.

                        "What do you mean?" said Lodge
And, as he spoke, there was a sudden hush,
A tall gaunt woman with great burning eyes,
And white hair blown back softly from a face
Ethereally fierce, as might have looked
Cassandra in old age, stood at the door.
"Where is my Ben?" she said.

                           "Mother!" cried Ben.
He rose and caught her in his mighty arms.
Her labour-reddened, large-boned hands entwined
Behind his neck.

                    "She brought this to the gaol,"

Said Chapman quietly, tossing a phial across
To Camden. "And he meant to take it, too!
Before the hangman touched him. Half an hour
And you'd have been too late to save big Ben.
He has lived too much in ancient Rome to love
A slit nose and the pillory. He'd have wrapped
His purple round him like an emperor.
I think she had another for herself."
"There's Roman blood in both," Dekker replied;
"Don't look. She is weeping now,"

                      And, while Ben held
That gaunt old body sobbing against his heart,
Dekker, to make her think they paid no heed,
Began to sing; and very softly now,
Full forty voices echoed the refrain:—

      The Cardinal's Hat is a very good inn,
         And so is the *Puritan's Head;*
      But I knew a sign of Wine, a Wine
         That is better when all is said.
      It is whiter than Venus, redder than Mars,
         It was old when the world begun;
      For all good inns are moons or stars
         But the *Mermaid* is their Sun.

Chorus: They are all alight like moons in the night,
         But the *Mermaid* is their Sun.

      Therefore, when priest or parson cries
         That inns like flowers increase,
      I say that mine inn is a church likewise,
         And I say to them "Be at peace!"

An host may gather in dark St. Paul's
　　To salve their souls from sin;
But the Light may be where " two or three "
　　Drink Wine in the *Mermaid Inn*.

Chorus:　The Light may be where " two or three "
　　Drink Wine in the *Mermaid Inn*.

VII

THE BURIAL OF A QUEEN

VII

THE BURIAL OF A QUEEN

'TWAS on an All Souls' Eve that our good Inn
    — Whereof, for ten years now, myself was host —
Heard and took part in its most eerie tale.
  It was a bitter night; and master Ben,
— His hair now flecked with grey, though youth still fired
His deep and ageless eyes,— in the old oak-chair,
Over the roaring hearth, puffed at his pipe;
A little sad, as often I found him now
Remembering vanished faces. Yet the years
Brought others round him. Wreaths of Heliochrise
Gleamed still in that great tribe of Benjamin,
Burned still across the malmsey and muscadel.
Chapman and Browne, Herrick,—a name like thyme
Crushed into sweetness by a bare-foot maid
Milking, at dewy dawn, in Elfin-land,—
These three came late, and sat in a little room
Aside, supping together, on one great pie,
Whereof both crust and coffin were prepared
By master Herrick's receipt, and all washed down
With mighty cups of sack. This left with Ben,
John Ford, wrapped in his cloak, brooding aloof,
Drayton and Lodge and Drummond of Hawthornden.

Suddenly, in the porch, I heard a sound
Of iron that grated on the flags.   A spade
And pick came edging through the door.
                                    " O, room!
Room for the master-craftsman," muttered Ford,
And grey old sexton Scarlet hobbled in.
    He shuffled off the snow that clogged his boots,
— On my clean rushes!— brushed it from his cloak
Of Northern Russet, wiped his rheumatic knees,
Blew out his lanthorn, hung it on a nail,
Leaned his rude pick and spade against the wall,
Flung back his rough frieze hood, flapped his gaunt arms,
    " Plenty of work, eh Timothy?" said Ben.
And called for ale.
                        " Come to the fire," said Lodge.
" Room for the wisest counsellor of kings,
The kindly sage that puts us all to bed,
And tucks us up beneath the grass-green quilt."
" Work? Where's my liquor? O, ay, there's work to
        spare,"
Old Scarlet croaked, then quaffed his creaming stoup,
While Ben said softly —" Pity you could not spare,
You and your Scythe-man, some of the golden lads
That I have seen here in the Mermaid Inn!"
Then, with a quiet smile he shook his head
And turned to master Drummond of Hawthornden.
" Well, songs are good; but flesh and blood are better.
The grey old tomb of Horace glows for me
Across the centuries, with one little fire
Lit by a careless hand."   Then, under breath,
Yet with some passion, he murmured this brief rhyme:—

I

Dulce ridentem, laughing through the ages,
  Dulce loquentem, O, fairer far to me,
Rarer than the wisdom of all his golden pages
  Floats the happy laughter of his vanished Lalage.

II

Dulce loquentem,— we hear it and we know it.
  Dulce ridentem,— so musical and low.
"Mightier than marble is my song!" Ah, did the poet
  Know why little Lalage was mightier even so?

III

Dulce ridentem,— through all the years that sever,
  Clear as o'er yon hawthorn hedge we heard her passing
    by,—
Lalagen amabo,— a song may live for ever
  Dulce loquentem,— but Lalage must die.

"I'd like to learn that rhyme," the sexton said.
"I've a fine memory too. You start me now,
I'd keep it up all night with ancient ballads."
  And then — a strange thing happened. I saw John Ford
"With folded arms and melancholy hat"
(As in our Mermaid jest he still would sit)
Watching old Scarlet like a man in trance.
The Sexton gulped his ale and smacked his lips,
Then croaked again —"O, ay, there's work to spare,
We fills 'em faster than the spades can dig."
And, all at once, the lights burned low and blue.

Ford leaned right forward, with his grim black eyes
Widening.
                "Why, that's a marvellous ring!" he said,
And pointed to the sexton's gnarled old hand
Spread on that black oak-table like the claw
Of some great bird of prey. "A ruby worth
The ransom of a queen!" The fire leapt up!
The sexton stared at him;
Then stretched his hand out, with its blue-black nails,
Full in the light, a grim earth-coloured hand,
But bare as it was born.
                "There was a ring!
I could have sworn it! Red as blood!" cried Ford.
And Ben and Lodge and Drummond of Hawthornden
All stared at him. For such a silent soul
Was master Ford that, when he suddenly spake,
It struck the rest as dumb as if the Sphinx
Had opened its cold stone lips. He would sit mute
Brooding, aloof, for hours, his cloak around him,
A staff between his knees, as if prepared
For a long journey, a lonely pilgrimage
To some dark tomb; a strange and sorrowful soul,
Yet not — as many thought him — harsh or hard,
But of a most kind patience. Though he wrote
In blood, they say, the blood came from his heart;
And all the sufferings of this world he took
To his own soul, and bade them pasture there;
Till out of his compassion, he became
A monument of bitterness. He rebelled;
And so fell short of that celestial height
Whereto the greatest only climb, who stand

[136]

By Shakespeare, and accept the Eternal Law.
These find, in law, firm footing for the soul,
The strength that binds the stars, and reins the sea,
The base of being, the pillars of the world,
The pledge of honour, the pure cord of love,
The form of truth, the golden floors of heaven.
These men discern a height beyond all heights,
A depth below all depths, and never an end
Without a pang beyond it, and a hope;
Without a heaven beyond it, and a hell.
For these, despair is like a bubble pricked,
An old romance to make young lovers weep.
For these, the law becomes a fiery road,
A Jacob's ladder through that vast abyss,
Lacking no rung from realm to loftier realm,
Nor wanting one degree from dust to wings.
These, at the last, radiant with victory,
Lay their strong hands upon the wingéd steeds
And fiery chariots, and exult to hold,
Themselves, the throbbing reins, whereby they steer
The stormy splendours.
                              He, being less, rebelled,
Cried out for unreined steeds, and unruled stars,
An unprohibited ocean and a truth
Untrue; and the equal thunder of the law
Hurled him to night and chaos, who was born
To shine upon the forehead of the day.
And yet — the voice of darkness and despair
May speak for heaven where heaven would not be heard,
May fight for heaven where heaven would not prevail,
And the consummate splendour of that strife,

Swallowing up all discords, all defeat,
In one huge victory, harmonising all,
Make Lucifer, at last, at one with God.

There,—on that All Souls' Eve, you might have thought
A dead man spoke, to see how Drayton stared,
And Drummond started.

              "You saw no ruby ring,"
The old sexton muttered sullenly. "If you did,
The worse for me, by all accounts. The lights
Burned low. You caught the fire-light on my fist.
What was it like, this ring?"

                "A band of gold,
And a great ruby, heart-shaped, fit to burn
Between the breasts of Laïs. Am I awake
Or dreaming?"

            "Well,—that makes the second time!
There's many have said they saw it, out of jest,
To scare me. For the astrologer did say
The third time I should die. Now, did you see it?
Most likely someone's told you that old tale!
You hadn't heard it, now?"

            Ford shook his head.

"What tale?" said Ben.

           "O, you could make a book
About my life. I've talked with quick and dead,
And neither ghost nor flesh can fright me now!
I wish it was a ring, so's I could catch him,
And sell him; but I've never seen him yet.
A white witch told me, if I did, I'd go
Clink, just like that, to heaven or t'other place,

MICHAEL DRAYTON

From an Original Painting in Dulwich College

Whirled in a fiery chariot with ten steeds
The way Elijah went. For I have seen
So many mighty things that I must die
Mightily.
        Well,— I came, sirs, to my craft
The day mine uncle Robert dug the grave
For good Queen Katharine, she whose heart was broke
By old King Harry, a very great while ago.
Maybe you've heard about my uncle, sirs?
He was far-famed for his grave-digging.
In depth, in speed, in neatness, he'd no match!
They've put a fine slab to his memory
In Peterborough Cathedral — *Robert Scarlet,*
Sexton for half a century, it says,
In Peterborough Cathedral, where he built
The last sad habitation for two queens,
And many hundreds of the common sort.
And now himself, who for so many built
Eternal habitations, others have buried.
Obiit anno ætatis, ninety-eight,
July the second, fifteen ninety-four.
  We should do well, sir, with a slab like that,
Shouldn't we? " And the sexton leered at Lodge.
" Not many boasts a finer slab than that,
There's many a king done worse. Ah, well, you see,
He'd a fine record. Living to ninety-eight,
He buried generations of the poor,
A countless host, and thought no more of it
Than digging potatoes. He'd a lofty mind
That found no satisfaction in small deeds.
But from his burying of two queens he drew

A lively pleasure. Could he have buried a third,
It would indeed have crowned his old white hairs.
But he was famous, and he thought, perchance,
A third were mere vain-glory. So he died.
I helped him with the second."

                    The old man leered
To see the shaft go home.

                    Ben filled the stoup
With ale. "So that," quoth he, "began the tale
About this ruby ring?" "But who," said Lodge,
"Who was the second queen?"

                    "A famous queen,
And a great lover! When you hear her name,
Your hearts will leap. Her beauty passed the bounds
Of modesty, men say, yet — she died young!
We buried her at midnight. There were few
That knew it; for the high State Funeral
Was held upon the morrow, Lammas morn.
Anon you shall hear why. A strange thing that,—
To see the mourners weeping round a hearse
That held a dummy coffin. Stranger still
To see us lowering the true coffin down
By torchlight, with some few of her true friends,
In Peterborough Cathedral, all alone."

  "Old as the world," said Ford. "It is the way
Of princes. Their true tears and smiles are seen
At dead of night, like ghosts raised from the grave!
And all the luxury of their brief, bright noon,
Cloaks but a dummy throne, a mask of life;
And, at the last, drapes a false catafalque,
Holding a vacant urn, a mask of death.

But tell, tell on!"

                The sexton took a draught
Of ale and smacked his lips.

                      " Mine uncle lived
A mile or more from Peterborough then.
And, past his cottage, in the dead of night,
Her royal coach came creeping through the lanes,
With scutcheons round it and no crowd to see,
And heralds carrying torches in their hands,
And none to admire, but him and me, and one,
A pedlar-poet, who lodged with us that week
And paid his lodging with a bunch of rhymes.
By these, he said, my uncle Robert's fame
Should live, as in a picture, till the crack
Of doom. My uncle thought that he should pay
Four-pence beside; but, when the man declared
The thought unworthy of these august events,
My uncle was abashed.

                And, truth to tell,
The rhymes were mellow, though here and there he swerved
From truth to make them so. Nor would he change
' June' to ' July' for all that we could say.
' I never said the month was June,' he cried,
' And if I did, Shakespeare hath jumped an age!
Gods, will you hedge me round with thirty nights?
" June " rhymes with " moon "!' With that, he flung them
          down
And strode away like Lucifer, and was gone,
Before old Scarlet could approach again
The matter of that four-pence.

                   Yet his rhymes
Have caught the very colours of that night!
I can see through them,
Ay, just as through our cottage window-panes,
Can see the great black coach,
Carrying the dead queen past our garden-gate.
The roses bobbing and fluttering to and fro,
Hide, and yet show the more by hiding, half.
And, like smoked glass through which you see the sun,
The song shows truest when it blurs the truth.
This is the way it goes."
                He rose to his feet,
Picked up his spade, and struck an attitude,
Leaning upon it. "I've got to feel my spade,
Or I'll forget it. This is the way I speak it.
Always." And, with a schoolboy's rigid face,
And eyes fixed on the rafters, he began,
Sing-song, the pedlar-poet's bunch of rhymes:—

    As I went by the cattle-shed
      The grey dew dimmed the grass,
    And, under a twisted apple-tree,
    Old Robin Scarlet stood by me.
    "Keep watch! Keep watch to-night," he said,
      "There's things 'ull come to pass.

    "Keep watch until the moon has cleared
      The thatch of yonder rick;
    Then I'll come out of my cottage-door
    To wait for the coach of a queen once more;
    And — you'll say nothing of what you've heard,
      But rise and follow me quick."

[142]

" And what 'ull I see if I keep your trust,
    And wait and watch so late? "
" Pride," he said, " and Pomp," he said,
" Beauty to haunt you till you're dead,
And Glorious Dust that goes to dust,
    Passing the white farm-gate.

" You are young and all for adventure, lad,
    And the great tales to be told:
This night, before the clock strike one,
Your lordliest hour will all be done;
But you'll remember it and be glad,
    In the days when you are old! "

All in the middle of the night,
    My face was at the pane;
When, creeping out of his cottage-door,
To wait for the coach of a queen once more,
Old Scarlet, in the moon-light,
    Beckoned to me again.

He stood beneath a lilac-spray,
    Like Father Time for dole,
In Reading Tawny cloak and hood,
With mattock and with spade he stood,
And, far away to southward,
    A bell began to toll.

He stood beneath a lilac-spray,
    And never a word he said;
But, as I stole out of the house,

[143]

He pointed over the orchard boughs,
Where, not with dawn or sunset,
  The Northern sky grew red.

I followed him, and half in fear,
  To the old farm-gate again;
And, round the curve of the long white road,
I saw that the dew-dashed hedges glowed
Red with the grandeur drawing near,
  And the torches of her train.

They carried her down with singing,
  With singing sweet and low,
Slowly round the curve they came,
Twenty torches dropping flame,
The heralds that were bringing her
  The way we all must go.

'Twas master William Dethick,
  The Garter King of Arms,
Before her royal coach did ride,
With none to see his Coat of Pride,
For peace was on the country-side,
  And sleep upon the farms;

Peace upon the red farm,
  Peace upon the grey,
Peace on the heavy orchard trees,
And little white-walled cottages,
Peace upon the wayside,
  And sleep upon the way.

THE BURIAL OF A QUEEN

So master William Dethick,
   With forty horse and men,
Like any common man and mean
Rode on before the Queen, the Queen,
And — only a wandering pedlar
   Could tell the tale again.

How, like a cloud of darkness,
   Between the torches moved
Four black steeds and a velvet pall
Crowned with the Crown Imperiall
And — on her shield — the lilies,
   The lilies that she loved.

Ah, stained and ever stainless,
   Ah, white as her own hand,
White as the wonder of that brow,
Crowned with colder lilies now,
White on the velvet darkness,
   The lilies of her land!

The witch from over the water,
   The fay from over the foam,
The bride that rode thro' Edinbro' town
With satin shoes and a silken gown,
A queen, and a great king's daughter,—
   Thus they carried her home,

With torches and with scutcheons,
   Unhonoured and unseen,
With the lilies of France in the wind a-stir,

And the Lion of Scotland over her,
Darkly, in the dead of night,
They carried the Queen, the Queen!

The sexton paused and took a draught of ale.
" 'Twas there," he said, " I joined 'em at the gate,
My uncle and the pedlar. What they sang,
The little shadowy throng of men that walked
Behind the scutcheoned coach with bare bent heads
I know not; but 'twas very soft and low.
They walked behind the rest, like shadows flung
Behind the torch-light, from that strange dark hearse.
And, some said, afterwards, they were the ghosts
Of lovers that this queen had brought to death.
A foolish thought it seemed to me, and yet
Like the night-wind they sang. And there was one
An olive-coloured man,— the pedlar said
Was like a certain foreigner that she loved,
One Chastelard, a wild French poet of hers.
Also the pedlar thought they sang ' farewell '
In words like this and that the words in French
Were written by the hapless Queen herself,
When as a girl she left the vines of France
For Scotland and the halls of Holyrood:—

I

Though thy hands have plied their trade
Eighty years without a rest,
Robin Scarlet, never thy spade
Built a house for such a guest!

[146]

Carry her where, in earliest June,
  All the whitest hawthorns blow;
Carry her under the midnight moon,
  Singing very soft and low.
Slow between the low green larches, carry the lovely lady
    sleeping,
  Past the low white moon-lit farms, along the lilac-
    shadowed way!
Carry her through the summer darkness, weeping, weeping,
    weeping, weeping!
  Answering only, to any that ask you, whence ye carry her,
    —*Fotheringhay*!

II.

She was gayer than a child!
  —*Let your torches droop for sorrow.*—
Laughter in her eyes ran wild!
  —*Carry her down to Peterboro'.*—
Words were kisses in her mouth!
  —*Let no word of blame be spoken.*—
She was Queen of all the South!
  —*In the North, her heart was broken.*—
They should have left her in her vineyards, left her heart to
    her land's own keeping,
  Left her white breast room to breathe, and left her light
    foot free to dance.
Out of the cold grey Northern mists, we carry her weep-
    ing, weeping, weeping,—
        O, ma patrie,
        La plus chérie,
    Adieu, plaisant pays de France!

[147]

III

Many a red heart died to beat
— *Music swelled in Holyrood!* —
Once, beneath her fair white feet.
— *Now the floors may rot with blood* —
She was young and her deep hair —
— *Wind and rain were all her fate!* —
Trapped young Love as in a snare.
— *And the wind's a sword in the Canongate!*
Edinboro'!
Edinboro'!
*Music built the towers of Troy, but thy gray walls are built
of sorrow!*
Wind-swept hills, and sorrowful glens, of thrifty sowing
and iron reaping,
What if her foot were fair as a sunbeam, how should it
touch or melt your snows?
What if her hair were a silken mesh?
Hands of steel can deal hard blows,
Iron breast-plates bruise fair flesh!
Carry her southward, palled in purple,
Weeping, weeping, weeping, weeping,
What had their rocks to do with roses? Body and soul she
was all one rose.

Thus, through the summer night, slowly they went,
We three behind,— the pedlar-poet and I,
And Robin Scarlet. The moving flare that ringed
The escutcheoned hearse, lit every leaf distinct
Along the hedges and woke the sleeping birds,

But drew no watchers from the drowsier farms.
Thus, through a world of innocence and sleep,
We brought her to the doors of her last home,
In Peterborough Cathedral.   Round her tomb
They stood, in the huge gloom of those old aisles,
The heralds with their torches, but their light
Struggled in vain with that tremendous dark.
Their ring of smoky red could only show
A few sad faces round the purple pall,
The wings of a stone angel overhead,
The base of three great pillars, and, fitfully,
Faint as the phosphorus glowing in some old vault,
One little slab of marble, far away.

   Yet, or the darkness, or the pedlar's words
Had made me fanciful, I thought I saw
Bowed shadows praying in those unplumbed aisles,
Nay, dimly heard them weeping, in a grief
That still was built of silence, like the drip
Of water from a frozen fountain-head.

   We laid her in her grave.   We closed the tomb.
With echoing footsteps all the funeral went;
And I went last to close and lock the doors;
Last, and half frightened of the enormous gloom
That rolled along behind me as one by one
The torches vanished.   O, I was glad to see
The moon-light on the kind turf-mounds again.

   But, as I turned the key, a quivering hand
Was laid upon my arm.   I turned and saw
That foreigner with the olive-coloured face.

   From head to foot he shivered, as with cold.
He drew me into the shadows of the porch.

'Come back with me,' he whispered, and slid his hand
— Like ice it was! — along my wrist, and slipped
A ring upon my finger, muttering quick,
As in a burning fever, 'All the wealth
Of Eldorado for one hour! Come back!
I must go back and see her face again!
I was not there, not there, the day she — died.
You'll help me with the coffin. Not a soul
Will know. Come back! One moment, only one!'
　　I thought the man was mad, and plucked my hand
Away from him. He caught me by the sleeve,
And sank upon his knees, lifting his face
Most piteously to mine. 'One moment! See!
I loved her!'
I saw the moonlight glisten on his tears,
Great, long, slow tears they were; and then — my God —
As his face lifted and his head sank back
Beseeching me — I saw a crimson thread
Circling his throat, as though the headsman's axe
Had cloven it with one blow, so shrewd, so keen,
The head had slipped not from the trunk.
　　　　　　　　　　　　　　　　I gasped;

And, as he pleaded, stretching his head back,
The wound, O like a second awful mouth,
The wound began to gap.
　　　　　　　　　　　I tore my cloak
Out of his clutch. My keys fell with a clash.
I left them where they lay, and with a shout
I dashed into the broad white empty road.
There was no soul in sight. Sweating with fear
I hastened home, not daring to look back;

But as I turned the corner, I heard the clang
Of those great doors, and knew he had entered in.

Not till I saw before me in the lane
The pedlar and my uncle did I halt
And look at that which clasped my finger still
As with a band of ice.

                       My hand was bare!
I stared at it and rubbed it. Then I thought
I had been dreaming. There had been no ring!
The poor man I had left there in the porch,
Being a Frenchman, talked a little wild;
But only wished to look upon her grave.
And I — I was the madman! So I said
Nothing. But all the same, for all my thoughts,
I'd not go back that night to find the keys,
No, not for all the rubies in the crown
Of Prester John.

      .   .   .   .

                  The high State Funeral
Was held on Lammas Day. A wondrous sight
For Peterborough! For myself, I found
Small satisfaction in a catafalque
That carried a dummy coffin. None the less,
The pedlar thought that as a Solemn Masque,
Or Piece of Purple Pomp, the thing was good,
And worthy of a picture in his rhymes;
The more because he said it shadowed forth
The ironic face of Death.

                   The Masque, indeed
Began before we buried her. For a host

Of Mourners — Lords and Ladies — on Lammas eve
Panting with eagerness of pride and place,
Arrived in readiness for the morrow's pomp,
And at the Bishop's Palace they found prepared
A mighty supper for them, where they sat
All at one table. In a Chamber hung
With scutcheons and black cloth, they drank red wine
And feasted, while the torches and the Queen
Crept through the darkness of Northampton lanes.

At seven o'clock on Lammas Morn they woke,
After the Queen was buried; and at eight
The Masque set forth, thus pictured in the rhymes
With tolling bells, which on the pedlar's lips
Had more than paid his lodging: Thus he spake it,
Slowly, sounding the rhymes like solemn bells,
And tolling, in between, with lingering tongue: —

Toll! — From the Palace the Releevants creep, —
   A hundred poor old women, nigh their end,
Wearing their black cloth gowns, and on each head
An ell of snow-white holland which, some said,
                  Afterwards they might keep,
—*Ah, Toll!* — with nine new shillings each to spend,
   For all the trouble that they had, and all
   The sorrow of walking to this funeral.

Toll! — And the Mourning Cloaks in purple streamed
   Following, a long procession, two by two,
Her Household first. With these, Monsieur du Preau
Her French Confessor, unafraid to show

The golden Cross that gleamed
About his neck, warned what the crowd might do
Said *I will wear it, though I die for it!*
So subtle in malice was that Jesuit.

Toll! — Sir George Savile in his Mourner's Gown
Carried the solemn Cross upon a Field
Azure, and under it by a streamer borne
Upon a field of Gules, an Unicorn
Argent and, lower down,
A scrolled device upon a blazoned shield,
Which seemed to say — I AM SILENT TILL THE END! —
Toll! Toll! — IN MY DEFENCE, GOD ME DEFEND!

Toll! — and a hundred poor old men went by,
Followed by two great Bishops.—*Toll, ah toll!* —
Then, with White Staves and Gowns, four noble lords;
Then sixteen Scots and Frenchmen with drawn swords;
Then, with a Bannerol,
Sir Andrew Noel, lifting to the sky
The Great Red Lion. Then the Crown and Crest
Borne by a Herald on his glittering breast.

And now — ah now, indeed, the deep bell tolls! —
That empty Coffin, with its velvet pall,
Borne by six Gentlemen, under a canopy
Of purple, lifted by four knights, goes by.
The Crown Imperiall
Burns on the Coffin-head. Four Bannerols
On either side, uplifted by four squires,
Roll on the wind their rich heraldic fires.

Toll! The Chief Mourner — the fair Russell! — *toll!* —
  Countess of Bedford — *toll!* — they bring her now,
Weeping under a purple Cloth of State,
Till, halting there before the Minister Gate,
              Having in her control
The fair White Staves of office, with a bow
  She gives them to her two great Earls again,
  Then sweeps them onward in her mournful train.

Toll! At the high Cathedral door the Quires
  Meet them and lead them, singing all the while
A mighty *Miserere* for her soul!
Then, as the rolling organ — *toll, ah toll!* —
              Floods every glimmering aisle
With ocean-thunders, all those knights and squires
  Bring the false Coffin to the central nave
  And set it in the Catafalque o'er her grave.

The Catafalque was made in Field-bed wise
  Valanced with midnight purple, fringed with gold:
All the Chief Mourners on dark thrones were set
Within it, as jewels in some huge carcanet:
              Above was this device
IN MY DEFENCE, GOD ME DEFEND, inscrolled
  Round the rich Arms of Scotland, as to say
  "Man judged me. I abide the Judgment Day."

The sexton paused anew. All looked at him,
And at his wrinkled, grim, earth-coloured hand,
As if, in that dim light, beclouded now
With blue tobacco-smoke, they thought to see
The smouldering ruby again.

[154]

                   "Ye know," he said,
"How master William Wickham preached that day?"
Ford nodded. "I have heard of it. He showed
Subtly, O very subtly, after his kind,
That the white Body of Beauty such as hers
Was in itself Papistical, a feast,
A fast, an incense, a burnt-offering,
And an Abomination in the sight
Of all true Protestants. Why, her very name
Was Mary!"

            "Ay, that's true, that's very true!"
The sexton mused. "Now that's a strange deep thought!
The Bishop missed a text in missing that.
Her name, indeed, was Mary!"

                     "Did you find
Your keys again?" "Ay, sir, I found them!" "Where?"
"Strange you should ask me that! After the throng
Departed, and the Nobles were at feast,
All in the Bishop's Palace — a great feast
And worthy of their sorrow — I came back
Carrying my uncle's second bunch of keys
To lock the doors and search, too, for mine own.
'Twas growing dusk already, and as I thrust
The key into the lock, the great grey porch
Grew cold upon me, like a tomb.

                         I pushed
Hard at the key — then stopped — with all my flesh
Freezing, and half in mind to fly; for, sirs,
The door was locked already, and — *from within!*

I drew the key forth quietly and stepped back
Into the Churchyard, where the graves were warm
With sunset still, and the blunt carven stones
Lengthened their homely shadows, out and out,
To Everlasting.   Then I plucked up heart,
Seeing the foot-prints of that mighty Masque
Along the pebbled path.   A queer thought came
Into my head that all the world without
Was but a Masque, and I was creeping back,
Back from the Mourner's Feast to Truth again.
Yet — I grew bold, and tried the Southern door.

    'Twas locked, but held no key on the inner side
To foil my own, and softly, softly, click,
I turned it, and with heart, sirs, in my mouth,
Pushed back the studded door and entered in . . .

    Stepped straight out of the world, I might have said,
Out of the dusk into a night so deep,
So dark, I trembled like a child. . . .

                  And then
I was aware, sirs, of a great sweet wave
Of incense.   All the gloom was heavy with it,
As if her Papist Household had returned
To pray for her poor soul; and, my fear went.
But either that strange incense weighed me down,
Or else from being sorely over-tasked,
A languor came upon me, and sitting there
To breathe a moment, in a velvet stall,
I closed mine eyes.

           A moment, and no more,
For then I heard a rustling in the nave,
And opened them; and, very far away,

As if across the world, in Rome herself,
I saw twelve tapers in the solemn East,
And saw, or thought I saw, cowled figures kneel
Before them, in an incense-cloud.

                      And then,
Maybe the sunset deepened in the world
Of masques without — clear proof that I had closed
Mine eyes but for a moment, sirs, I saw
As if across a world-without-end tomb,
A tiny jewelled glow of crimson panes
Darkening and brightening with the West.

                        And then,
Then I saw something more — Queen Mary's vault,
And — it was open! . . .

                Then, I heard a voice,
A strange deep broken voice, whispering love
In soft French words, that clasped and clung like hands;
And then — two shadows passed against the West,
Two blurs of black against that crimson stain,
Slowly, O very slowly, with bowed heads,
Leaning together, and vanished into the dark
Beyond the Catafalque.

                Then — I heard him pray,—
And knew him for the man that prayed to me,—
Pray as a man prays for his love's last breath!
And then, O sirs, it caught me by the throat,
And I, too, dropped upon my knees and prayed;
For, as in answer to his prayer, there came
A moan of music, a mighty shuddering sound
From the great organ, a sound that rose and fell
Like seas in anger, very far away;

And then a peal of thunder, and then it seemed,
As if the graves were giving up their dead,
A great cowled host of shadows rose and sang:—

> *Dies iræ, dies illâ*
> *Solvet sæclum in favilla,*
> *Teste David cum Sibylla.*

I heard her sad, sad, little, broken voice,
Out in the darkness. 'Ay, and David, too,
His blood is on the floors of Holyrood,
To speak for me.' Then that great ocean-sound
Swelled to a thunder again, and heaven and earth
Shrivelled away; and in that huge slow hymn
Chariots were driven forth in flaming rows,
And terrible trumpets blown from deep to deep.

And then, ah then, the heart of heaven was hushed,
And — in the hush — it seemed an angel wept,
Another Mary wept, and gathering up
All our poor wounded, weary, way-worn world,
Even as a Mother gathers up her babe,
Soothed it against her breast, and rained her tears
On the pierced feet of God, and melted Him
To pity, and over His feet poured her deep hair.
The music died away. The shadows knelt.
And then — I heard a rustling nigh the tomb,
And heard — and heard — or dreamed I heard — farewells,
Farewells for everlasting, deep farewells,
Bitter as blood, darker than any death.
And, at the last, as in a kiss, one breath,

One agony of sweetness, like a sword
For sharpness, drawn along a soft white throat;
And, for its terrible sweetness, like a sigh
Across great waters, very far away,—
Sweetheart!
And then, like doors, like world-without-end doors
That shut for Everlasting, came a clang,
And ringing, echoing, through the echo of it,
One terrible cry that plucked my heart-strings out,
Mary! And on the closed and silent tomb,
Where there were two, one shuddering shadow lay,
And then — I, too,— reeled, swooned and knew no more.

Sirs, when I woke, there was a broad bright shaft
Of moonlight, slanting through an Eastern pane
Full on her tomb and that black Catafalque.
And on the tomb there lay — my bunch of keys!
I struggled to my feet,
Ashamed of my wild fancies, like a man
Awakening from a drunken dream. And yet,
When I picked up the keys, although that storm
Of terror had all blown by and left me calm,
I lifted up mine eyes to see the scroll
Round the rich crest of that dark canopy,
IN MY DEFENCE, GOD ME DEFEND. The moon
Struck full upon it; and, as I turned and went,
God help me, sirs, though I were loyal enough
To good Queen Bess, I could not help but say,
Amen!
And yet, methought it was not I that spake,
But some deep soul that used me for a mask,

A soul that rose up in this hollow shell
Like dark sea-tides flooding an empty cave.
I could not help but say with my poor lips,
Amen! Amen!
                    Sirs, 'tis a terrible thing
To move in great events.   Since that strange night
I have not been as other men.   The tides
Would rise in this dark cave "— he tapped his skull —
" Deep tides, I know not whence; and when they rose
My friends looked strangely upon me and stood aloof.
And once, my uncle said to me — indeed,
It troubled me strangely,— ' Timothy,' he said,
' Thou art translated!   I could well believe
Thou art two men, whereof the one's a fool,
The other a prophet.   Or else, beneath thy skin
There lurks a changeling!   What hath come to thee?'
And then, sirs, then — well I remember it!
'Twas on a summer eve, and we walked home
Between high ghostly hedges white with may —
And uncle Robin, in his holy-day suit
Of Reading Tawny, felt his old heart swell
With pride in his great memories.   He began
Chanting the pedlar's tune, keeping the time
Thus, jingle, jingle, slowly, with his keys:—

I

Douglas, in the moonless night
    — *Muffled oars on blue Loch Leven!* —
Took her hand, a flake of white
    — *Beauty slides the bolts of heaven.* —

[160]

Little white hand, like a flake of snow,
　　When they saw it, his Highland crew
Swung together and murmured low,
　　"Douglas, wilt *thou* die then, too?"
And the pine trees whispered weeping
　　"Douglas, Douglas, tender and true!
Little white hand like a tender moon-beam, soon shall you
　　　　set the broad-swords leaping.
　It is the Queen, the Queen!" they whispered, watching
　　　　her soar to the saddle anew.
"There will be trumpets blown in the mountains, a mist
　　　　of blood on the heather, and weeping,
　　Weeping, weeping, and *thou,* too, dead for her, Douglas,
　　　　Douglas, tender and true."

II

　Carry the queenly lass along!
　　　— Cold she lies, cold and dead,—
　She whose laughter was a song,
　　　— Lapped around with sheets of lead!—
　She whose blood was wine of the South,
　　　— Light her down to a couch of clay!—
　And a royal rose her mouth,
　　　And her body made of may!
　— Lift your torches, weeping, weeping,
　　　Light her down to a couch of clay.
They should have left her in her vineyards, left her heart
　　　　to her land's own keeping,
　　Left her white breast room to breathe, and left her light
　　　　foot free to dance!

Hush! Between the solemn pinewoods, carry the lovely
      lady sleeping,
  Out of the cold grey Northern mists, with banner and
      scutcheon, plume, and lance,
Carry her southward, palled in purple, weeping, weeping,
      weeping, weeping,—

> *O, ma patrie,*
> *La plus chérie,*
> *Adieu, plaisant pays de France!*

Well, sirs, that dark tide rose within my brain!
I snatched his keys and flung them over the hedge,
Then flung myself down on a bank of ferns
And wept and wept and wept.
                                        It puzzled him.
Perchance he feared my mind was going and yet,
O, sirs, if you consider it rightly now,
With all those ages knocking at his doors,
With all that custom clamouring for his care,
Is it so strange a grave-digger should weep?
Well — he was kind enough and heaped my plate
That night at supper.
But I could never dig my graves at ease
In Peterborough Churchyard. So I came
To London — to St. Mary Magdalen's.
And thus, I chanced to drink my ale one night
Here in the Mermaid Inn. 'Twas All Souls' Eve,
And, on that bench, where master Ford now sits
Was master Shakespeare—
Well, the lights burned low,
And just like master Ford to-night he leaned

Suddenly forward. "Timothy," he said,
"That's a most marvellous ruby!"

My blood froze!
I stretched my hand out bare as it was born;
And he said nothing, only looked at me.
Then, seeing my pipe was empty, he bade me fill
And lit it for me.

Peach, the astrologer,
Was living then; and that same night I went
And told him all my trouble about this ring.
He took my hand in his, and held it — thus —
Then looked into my face and said this rhyme:—

> *The ruby ring, that only three*
> *While Time and Tide go by, shall see,*
> *Weds your hand to history.*
>
> *Honour and pride the first shall lend;*
> *The second shall give you gold to spend;*
> *The third — shall warn you of your end.*

Peach was a rogue, some say, and yet he spake
Most truly about the first," the sexton mused,
"For master Shakespeare, though they say in youth,
Outside the theatres, he would hold your horse
For pence, prospered at last, bought a fine house
In Stratford, lived there like a squire, they say.
And here, here he would sit, for all the world
As he were but a poet! God bless us all,
And then — to think!— he rose to be a squire!
A deep one, masters! Well, he lit my pipe!"

"Why did they bury such a queen by night?"
Said Ford. "Kings might have wept for her. Did Death
Play epicure and glutton that so few
Were bidden to such a feast. Once on a time,
I could have wept, myself, to hear a tale
Of beauty buried in the dark. And hers
Was loveliness, far, far beyond the common!
Such beauty should be marble to the touch
Of time, and clad in purple to amaze
The moth. But she was kind and soft and fair,
A woman, and so she died. But, why the dark?"

"Sir, they gave out the coffin was too heavy
For gentlemen to bear!"—"For kings to bear?"
Ford flashed at him. The sexton shook his head,—
"Nay! Gentlemen to bear! But — the true cause —
Ah, sir, 'tis unbelievable, even to me,
A sexton, for a queen so fair of face!
And all her beds, even as the pedlar said,
Breathing Arabia, sirs, her walls all hung
With woven purple wonders and great tales
Of amorous gods, and mighty mirrors, too,
Imaging her own softness, night and dawn,
When through her sumptuous hair she drew the combs;
And like one great white rose-leaf half her breast
Shone through it, firm as ivory."
                                        "Ay," said Lodge,
Murmuring his own rich music under breath,
"*About her neck did all the graces throng,*
And lay such baits as did entangle death."

"Well, sir, the weather being hot, they feared
She would not hold the burying!" . . .
                                    "In some sort,"
Ford answered slowly, "if your tale be true,
She did not hold it. Many a knightly crest
Will bend yet o'er the ghost of that small hand."

There was a hush, broken by Ben at last,
Who turned to Ford —"How now, my golden lad?
The astrologer's dead hand is on thy purse!"

Ford laughed, grimly, and flung an angel down.
"Well, cause or consequence, rhyme or no rhyme,
There is thy gold. I will not break the spell,
Or thou mayst live to bury us one and all!"
  "And, if I live so long," the old man replied,
Lighting his lanthorn, "you may trust me, sirs,
Mine Inn is quiet, and I can find you beds
Where Queens might sleep all night and never move.
Good-night, sirs, and God bless you, one and all."
  He shouldered pick and spade. I opened the door.
The snow blew in, and, as he shuffled out,
There, in the strait dark passage, I could swear
I saw a spark of red upon his hand,
Like a great smouldering ruby.
                              I gasped. He stopped.
He peered at me.
                  "Twice in a night," he said.
"Nothing," I answered, "only the lanthorn-light."
He shook his head. "I'll tell you something more!
There's nothing, nothing now in life or death

That frightens me. Ah, things used to frighten me.
But never now. I thought I had ten years;
But if the warning comes and says ' *Thou fool,*
This night! ' Why, then, I'm ready."

I watched him go,

With glimmering lanthorn up the narrow street,
Like one that walked upon the clouds, through snow
That seemed to mix the City with the skies.

On Christmas Eve we heard that he was dead.

VIII

FLOS MERCATORUM

VIII

FLOS MERCATORUM

FLOS MERCATORUM! On that night of nights
    We drew from our Mermaid cellarage
All the old glory of London in one cask
Of magic vintage. Never a city on earth —
Rome, Paris, Florence, Bagdad — held for Ben
The colours of old London; and, that night,
We staved them like a wine, and drank, drank deep!

'Twas Master Heywood, whom the Mermaid Inn
Had dubbed our London laureate, hauled the cask
Out of its ancient harbourage. " Ben," he cried,
Bustling into the room with Dekker and Brome,
" The prentices are up! " Ben raised his head
Out of the chimney-corner where he drowsed,
And listened, reaching slowly for his pipe.

" *Clerk of the Bow Bell,*" all along the Cheape
There came a shout that swelled into a roar.
    " What! Will they storm the Mermaid? " Heywood
        laughed,
" They are turning into Bread Street! "
                                    Down they came!
We heard them hooting round the poor old Clerk —
" Clubs! Clubs! The rogue would have us work all night!

He rang ten minutes late! Fifteen, by Paul's! "
And over the hubbub rose, like a thin bell,
The Clerk's entreaty —" Now, good boys, good boys,
Children of Cheape, be still, I do beseech you!
I took some forty winks, but then . . ." A roar
Of wrathful laughter drowned him —" Forty winks!
Remember Black May-day! We'll make you wink! "
There was a scuffle, and into the tavern rushed
Gregory Clopton, Clerk of the Bow Bell,—
A tall thin man, with yellow hair a-stream,
And blazing eyes.

         " Hide me," he clamoured, " quick!
These picaroons will murder me! "

             I closed
The thick oak doors against the coloured storm
Of prentices in red and green and ray,
Saffron and Reading tawny. Twenty clubs
Drubbed on the panels as I barred them out;
And even our walls and shutters could not drown
Their song that, like a mocking peal of bells,
Under our windows, made all Bread Street ring:—

> *" Clerk of the Bow Bell,*
>   *With the yellow locks,*
> *For thy late ringing*
>   *Thy head shall have knocks!"*

Then Heywood, seeing the Clerk was all a-quake,
Went to an upper casement that o'er-looked
The whole of Bread Street. Heywood knew their ways,
And parleyed with them till their anger turned

FRANCIS BEAUMONT

To shouts of merriment.   Then, like one deep bell
His voice rang out, in answer to their peal:—

> *" Children of Cheape,*
> *Hold you all still!*
> *You shall have Bow Bell*
> *Rung at your will! "*

Loudly they cheered him.   Courteously he bowed,
Then firmly shut the window; and, ere I filled
His cup with sack again, the crowd had gone.

" My clochard, sirs, is warm," quavered the Clerk.
" I do confess I took some forty winks!
They are good lads, our prentices of Cheape,
But hasty! "
              " Wine! " said Ben.   He filled a cup
And thrust it into Gregory's trembling hands.
" Yours is a task," said Dekker, " a great task!
You sit among the gods, a lord of time,
Measuring out the pulse of London's heart."
  " Yea, sir, above the hours and days and years,
I sometimes think.   'Tis a great Bell — the Bow!
And hath been, since the days of Whittington."
  " The good old days," growled Ben.   " Both good and
        bad
Were measured by my Bell," the Clerk replied.
And, while he spoke, warmed by the wine, his voice
Mellowed and floated up and down the scale
As if the music of the London bells
Lingered upon his tongue.   " I know them all,
And love them, all the voices of the bells.

[171]

FLOS MERCATORUM! That's the Bell of Bow
Remembering Richard Whittington. You should hear
The bells of London when they tell his tale.
Once, after hearing them, I wrote it down.
I know the tale by heart now, every turn."
　"Then ring it out," said Heywood.
　　　　　　　　　　　　　　　　Gregory smiled
And cleared his throat.
　　　　　　　　　　　　"You must imagine, sirs,
The Clerk, sitting on high, among the clouds,
With London spread beneath him like a map.
Under his tower, a flock of prentices
Calling like bells, of little size or weight,
But bells no less, ask that the Bell of Bow
Shall tell the tale of Richard Whittington,
As thus."
　　　　　　Then Gregory Clopton, mellowing all
The chiming vowels, and dwelling on every tone
In rhythm or rhyme that helped to swell the peal
Or keep the ringing measure, beat for beat,
Chanted this legend of the London bells:—

Clerk of the Bow Bell, four and twenty prentices,
　All upon a Hallowe'en, we prithee, for our joy,
Ring a little turn again for sweet Dick Whittington,
　Flos Mercatorum, and a barefoot boy!—

"Children of Cheape," did that old Clerk answer,
　"You will have a peal, then, for well may you know,
All the bells of London remember Richard Whittington
　When they hear the voice of the big Bell of Bow!"—

[172]

Clerk with the yellow locks, mellow be thy malmsey!
  He was once a prentice, and carolled in the Strand!
Ay, and we are all, too, Marchaunt Adventurers,
  Prentices of London, and lords of Engeland.

" Children of Cheape," did that old Clerk answer,
  " Hold you, ah hold you, ah hold you all still!
Souling if you come to the glory of a Prentice,
  You shall have the Bow Bell rung at your will! "

" Whittington! Whittington! O, turn again, Whittington,
  Lord Mayor of London," the big Bell began:
" Where was he born? O, at Pauntley in Gloucestershire
  Hard by Cold Ashton, Cold Ashton," it ran.

" *Flos Mercatorum,*" moaned the bell of All Hallowes,
  " There was he an orphan, O, a little lad alone! "
" Then we all sang," echoed happy St. Saviour's,
  " Called him, and lured him, and made him our own.

Told him a tale as he lay upon the hillside,
  Looking on his home in the meadow-lands below! "
" Told him a tale," clanged the bell of Cold Abbey;
  " Told him the truth," boomed the big Bell of Bow!

Sang of a City that was like a blazoned missal-book,
  Black with oaken gables, carven and inscrolled;
Every street a coloured page, every sign a hieroglyph,
  Dusky with enchantments, a City paved with gold;

" Younger son, younger son, up with stick and bundle! "—
  Even so we rung for him —" But — kneel before you go;

Watch by your shield, lad, in little Pauntley Chancel,
  Look upon the painted panes that hold your Arms a-
    glow,—

Coat of Gules and Azure; but the proud will not remember
    it!
  And the Crest a Lion's Head, until the new be won!
Far away, remember it! And O, remember this, too,—
  Every barefoot boy on earth is but a younger son."

Proudly he answered us, beneath the painted window,—
  "Though I be a younger son, the glory falls to me:
While my brother bideth by a little land in Gloucestershire,
  All the open Earth is mine, and all the Ocean-sea.

Yet will I remember, yet will I remember,
  By the chivalry of God, until my day be done,
When I meet a gentle heart, lonely and unshielded,
  Every barefoot boy on earth is but a younger son!"

Then he looked to Northward for the painted ships of
    Bristol;
  Far away, and cold as death, he saw the Severn shine:
Then he looked to Eastward, and he saw a string of colours
  Trickling through the grey hills, like elfin drops of wine;

Down along the Mendip dale, the chapmen and their horses,
  Far away, and carrying each its little coloured load,
Winding like a fairy-tale, with pack and corded bundle,
  Trickled like a crimson thread along the silver road.

Quick he ran to meet them, stick and bundle on his shoulder!
  Over by Cold Ashton, he met them trampling down,—
White shaggy horses with their packs of purple spicery,
  Crimson kegs of malmsey, and the silks of London town.

When the chapmen asked of him the bridle-path to Dorset,
  Blithely he showed them, and he led them on their way,
Led them through the fern with their bales of breathing
      Araby,
  Led them to a bridle-path that saved them half a day.

Merrily shook the silver bells that hung the broidered bridle-
      rein,
  Chiming to his hand, as he led them through the fern,
Down to deep Dorset, and the wooded Isle of Purbeck,
  Then — by little Kimmeridge — they led him turn for
      turn.

Down by little Kimmeridge, and up by Hampshire forest-
      roads,
  Round by Sussex violets, and apple-bloom of Kent,
Singing songs of London, telling tales of London,
  All the way to London, with packs of wool they went.

" London was London, then!   A clean, clear moat
Girdled her walls that measured, round about,
Three miles or less.   She is big and dirty now,"
Said Dekker.
            " Call it a silver moat," growled Ben,
" That's the new poetry!   Call it crystal, lad!
But, till you kiss the Beast, you'll never find

Your Fairy Prince. Why, all those crowded streets,
Flung all their filth, their refuse, rags and bones,
Dead cats and dogs, into your clean clear moat,
And made it sluggish as old Acheron.
Fevers and plagues, death in a thousand shapes
Crawled out of it. London was dirty, lad;
And till you kiss that fact, you'll never see
The glory of this old Jerusalem!"

"Ay, 'tis the fogs that make the sunset red,"
Answered Tom Heywood. "London is earthy, coarse,
Grimy and grand. You must make dirt the ground,
Or lose the colours of friend Clopton's tale.
Ring on!" And, nothing loth, the Clerk resumed:—

Bravely swelled his heart to see the moat of London glittering
  Round her mighty wall — they told him — two miles
   long!
Then — he gasped as, echoing in by grim black Aldgate,
  Suddenly their shaggy nags were nodding through a
   throng:

Prentices in red and ray, marchaunts in their saffron,
  Aldermen in violets, and minstrels in white,
Clerks in homely hoods of budge, and wives with crimson
   wimples,
Thronging as to welcome him that happy summer night.

"Back," they cried, and "Clear the way," and caught the
   ringing bridle-reins:
  "Wait! the Watch is going by, this vigil of St. John!"

Merrily laughed the chapmen then, reining their great white
      horses back,
  " When the pageant passes, lad, we'll up and follow on ! "

There, as thick the crowd surged, beneath the blossomed ale-
      poles,
  Lifting up to Whittington a fair face afraid,
Swept against his horse by a billow of madcap prentices,
  Hard against the stirrup breathed a green-gowned maid.

Swift he drew her up and up, and throned her there before
      him,
  High above the throng with her laughing April eyes,
Like a Queen of Faërie on the great pack-saddle.
  " Hey ! " laughed the chapmen, " the prentice wins the
      prize ! "

" Whittington ! Whittington ! the world is all before you ! "
  Blithely rang the bells and the steeples rocked and reeled !
Then — he saw her eyes grow wide, and, all along by
      Leaden Hall,
  Drums rolled, earth shook, and shattering trumpets
      pealed.

Like a marching sunset, there, from Leaden Hall to Aldgate,
  Flared the crimson cressets — O, her brows were haloed
      then !—
Then the stirring steeds went by with all their mounted
      trumpeters,
  Then, in ringing harness, a thousand marching men.

Marching — marching — his heart and all the halberdiers,
  And his pulses throbbing with the throbbing of the drums;
Marching — marching — his blood and all the burganets!
  " Look," she cried, " O, look," she cried, " and now the
      morrice comes! "

Dancing — dancing — her eyes and all the Lincoln Green,
  Robin Hood and Friar Tuck, dancing through the town!
" Where is Marian? " Laughingly she turned to Richard
      Whittington.
  " Here," he said, and pointed to her own green gown.

Dancing — dancing — her heart and all the morrice-bells!
  Then there burst a mighty shout from thrice a thousand
      throats!
Then, with all their bows bent, and sheaves of peacock
      arrows,
  Marched the tall archers in their white silk coats,

White silk coats, with the crest of London City
  Crimson on the shoulder, a sign for all to read,—
Marching — marching — and then the sworded henchmen,
  Then, William Walworth, on his great stirring steed.

Flos Mercatorum, ay, the fish-monger, Walworth,—
  He whose nets of silk drew the silver from the tide,
He who saved the king when the king was but a prentice,—
  Lord Mayor of London, with his sword at his side!

Burned with magic changes, his blood and all the pageantry;
  Burned with deep sea-changes, the wonder in her eyes;

Flos Mercatorum! 'Twas the rose-mary of Paphos,
  Reddening all the City for the prentice and his prize!

All the book of London, the pages of adventure,
  Passed before the prentice on that vigil of St. John:
Then the chapmen shook their reins,—" We'll ride behind
      the revelry,
  Round again to Cornhill! Up, and follow on!"

Riding on his pack-horse, above the shouting multitude,
  There she turned and smiled at him, and thanked him for
      his grace:
"Let me down by *Red Rose Lane,*" and, like a wave of
      twilight
  While she spoke, her shadowy hair — touched his tin-
      gling face.

When they came to *Red Rose Lane,* beneath the blossomed
      ale-poles,
  Light along his arm she lay, a moment, leaping down:
Then she waved " farewell " to him, and down the Lane he
      watched her
  Flitting through the darkness in her gay green gown.

All along the Cheape, as he rode among the chapmen,
  Round by *Black Friars,* to the *Two-Necked Swan*
Coloured like the sunset, prentices and maidens
  Danced for red roses on the vigil of St. John.

Over them were jewelled lamps in great black galleries,
  Garlanded with beauty, and burning all the night;

All the doors were shadowy with orpin and St. John's wort,
    Long fennel, green birch, and lilies of delight.

" He should have slept here at the Mermaid Inn,"
Said Heywood as the chanter paused for breath.
" What? Has our Mermaid sung so long? " cried Ben.
" Her beams are black enough. There was an Inn,"
Said Tom, " that bore the name; and through its heart
There flowed the right old purple. I like to think
It was the same, where Lydgate took his ease
After his hood was stolen; and Gower, perchance;
And, though he loved the *Tabard* for a-while,
I like to think the Father of us all,
The old Adam of English minstrelsy caroused
Here in the Mermaid Tavern. I like to think
Jolly Dan Chaucer, with his kind shrewd face
Fresh as an apple above his fur-fringed gown,
One plump hand sporting with his golden chain,
Looked out from that old casement over the sign,
And saw the pageant, and the shaggy nags,
With Whittington, and his green-gowned maid, go by.
    " O, very like," said Clopton, " for the bells
Left not a head indoors that night." He drank
A draught of malmsey — and thus renewed his tale:—

" *Flos Mercatorum,*" mourned the bell of All Hallowes,
    " There was he an orphan, O, a little lad alone,
Rubbing down the great white horses for a supper! "
    " True," boomed the Bow Bell, " his hands were his
        own! "

Where did he sleep?   On a plump white wool-pack,
  Open to the moon on that Vigil of St. John,
Sheltered from the dew, where the black-timbered gallery
  Frowned above the yard of the *Two-Necked Swan.*

Early in the morning, clanged the bell of St. Martin's,
  Early in the morning, with a groat in his hand,
Mournfully he parted with the jolly-hearted chapmen,
  Shouldered his bundle and walked into the *Strand;*

Walked into the *Strand,* and back again to *West Cheape,*
  Staring at the wizardry of every painted sign,
Dazed with the steeples and the rich heraldic cornices
  Drinking in the colours of the Cheape like wine.

All about the booths now, the parti-coloured prentices
  Fluted like a flock of birds along a summer lane,
Green linnets, red caps, and gay gold-finches,—
  *What d'ye lack, and what d'ye lack, and what d'ye lack
    again?*

" Buy my dainty doublets, cut on double taffetas,
  Buy my Paris thread," they cried, and caught him by the
    hand,
" Laces for your Heart's-Delight, and lawns to make her
    love you,
Cambric for her wimple, O, the finest in the land."

Ah, but he was hungry, foot-sore, weary,
  Knocking at the doors of the armourers that day!

What d'ye lack? they asked of him; but no man lacked a
    prentice:
  When he told them what he lacked, they frowned and
    turned away.

Hard was his bed that night, beneath a cruel archway,
  Down among the hulks, with his heart growing cold!
London is a rare town, but O, the streets of London,
  Red though their flints be, they are not red with gold.

Pale in the dawn, ere he marched on his adventure,
  Starving for a crust, did he kneel a-while again,
Then, upon the fourth night, he cried, O, like a wounded
    bird,
  Let me die, if die I must, in *Red Rose Lane.*

Like a little wounded bird he trailed through the darkness,
  Laid him on a door-step, and then — O, like a breath
Pitifully blowing out his life's little rush-light,
  Came a gush of blackness, a swoon deep as death.

Then he heard a rough voice! Then he saw a lanthorn!
  Then he saw a bearded face, and blindly wondered whose:
Then — a marchaunt's portly legs, with great Rose-Win-
    dows,
  Bigger than St. Paul's, he thought, embroidered on his
    shoes.

"Alice!" roared the voice, and then, O like a lilied angel,
  Leaning from the lighted door a fair face afraid,

Leaning over *Red Rose Lane,* O, leaning out of Paradise,
   Drooped the sudden glory of his green-crowned maid!

   .   .   .   .   .   .

" O, mellow be thy malmsey," grunted Ben,
Filling the Clerk another cup.

                                 " The peal,"
Quoth Clopton, " is not ended, but the pause
In ringing, chimes to a deep inward ear
And tells its own deep tale. Silence and sound,
Darkness and light, mourning and mirth,— no tale,
No painting, and no music, nay, no world,
If God should cut their fruitful marriage-knot.
A shallow sort to-day would fain deny
A hell, sirs, to this boundless universe.
To such I say ' no hell, no Paradise! '
Others would fain deny the topless towers
Of heaven, and make this earth a hell indeed.
To such I say, ' the unplumbed gulfs of grief
Are only theirs for whom the blissful chimes
Ring from those unseen heights.' This earth, mid-way,
Hangs like a belfry where the ringers grasp
Their ropes in darkness, each in his own place,
Each knowing, by the tune in his own heart,
Never by sight, when he must toss through heaven
The tone of his own bell. Those bounded souls
Have never heard our chimes! Why, sirs, myself
Simply by running up and down the scale
Descend to hell or soar to heaven. My bells
Height above height, deep below deep, respond!
Their scale is infinite. Dare I, for one breath,
Dream that one note hath crowned and ended all,

Sudden I hear, far, far above those clouds,
Like laughing angels, peal on golden peal,
Innumerable as drops of April rain,
Yet every note distinct, round as a pearl,
And perfect in its place, a chime of law,
Whose pure and boundless mere arithmetic
Climbs with my soul to God."

        Ben looked at him,
Gently. " Resume, old moralist," he said.
" On to thy marriage-bells! "

         " The fairy-tales
Are wiser than they know, sirs. All our woes
Lead on to those celestial marriage-bells.
The world's a-wooing; and the pure City of God
Peals for the wedding of our joy and pain!
This was well seen of Richard Whittington;
For only he that finds the London streets
Paved with red flints, at last shall find them paved
Like to the Perfect City, with pure gold.
Ye know the world! what was a London waif
To Hugh Fitzwarren's daughter? He was fed
And harboured; and the cook declared she lacked
A scullion. So, in Hugh Fitzwarren's house,
He turned the jack, and scoured the dripping-pan.
How could he hope for more?

       This Marchaunt's house
Was builded like a great high-gabled inn,
Square, with a galleried courtyard, such as now
The players use. Its rooms were rich and dim
With deep-set coloured panes and massy beams.
Its ancient eaves jutted o'er *Red Rose Lane*

Darkly, like eyebrows of a mage asleep.
Its oaken stair coiled upward through a dusk
Heavy with fume of scented woods that burned
To keep the Plague away,— a gloom to embalm
A Pharaoh, but to dull the cheek and eye
Of country lads like Whittington.

　　　　　　　　　　　　　　He pined
For wind and sunlight.　Yet he plied his task
Patient as in old tales of Elfin-land,
The young knight would unhelm his golden locks
And play the scullion, so that he might watch
His lady's eyes unknown, and oftener hear
Her brook-like laughter rippling overhead;
Her green gown, like the breath of Eden boughs,
Rustling nigh him.　And all day long he found
Sunshine enough in this.　But when at night
He crept into the low dark vaulted den,
The cobwebbed cellar, where the cook had strewn
The scullion's bed of straw (and none too thick
Lest he should sleep too long), he choked for breath;
And, like an old man hoarding up his life,
Fostered his glimmering rushlight as he sate
Bolt upright, while a horrible scurry heaved
His rustling bed, and bright black-beaded eyes
Peered at him from the crannies of the wall.
Then darkness whelmed him, and perchance he slept,—
Only to fight with night-mares and to fly
Down endless tunnels in a ghastly dream,
Hunted by horrible human souls that took
The shape of monstrous rats, great chattering snouts,
Vile shapes of shadowy cunning and grey greed,

That gnaw through beams, and undermine tall towns,
And carry the seeds of plague and ruin and death
Under the careless homes of sleeping men.
    Thus, in the darkness, did he wage a war
With all the powers of darkness. 'If the light
Do break upon me, by the grace of God,'
So did he vow, 'O, then will I remember,
Then, then, will I remember, ay, and help
To build that lovelier City which is paved
For rich and poor alike, with purest gold.'

Ah, sirs, he kept his vow. Ye will not smile
If, at the first, the best that he could do
Was with his first poor penny-piece to buy
A cat, and bring her home, under his coat
By stealth (or else that termagant, the cook,
Had drowned it in the water-butt, nor deemed
The water worse to drink). So did he quell
First his own plague, but bettered all the house.
Now, in those days, Marchaunt Adventurers
Shared with their prentices the happy chance
Of each new venture. Each might have his stake,
Little or great, upon the glowing tides
Of high romance that washed the wharfs of Thames;
And every lad in London had his groat
Or splendid shilling on some fair ship at sea.

So, on an April eve, Fitzwarren called
His prentices together; for, ere long,
The *Unicorn,* his tall new ship, must sail
Beyond the world to gather gorgeous webs

From Eastern looms, great miracles of silk
Dipt in the dawn by wizard hands of Ind;
Or, if they chanced upon that fabled coast
Where Sydon, river of jewels, like a snake
Slides down the gorge its coils of crimson fire,
Perchance a richer cargo,— rubies, pearls,
Or gold bars from the Gates of Paradise.
And many a moon, at least, a faërie foam
Would lap Blackfriars wharf, where London lads
Glazed in the sunset down that misty reach
For old black battered hulks and tattered sails
Bringing their dreams home from the uncharted sea.

And one flung down a groat — he had no more.
One staked a shilling, one a good French crown;
And one an angel, O, light-winged enough
To reach Cathay; and not a lad but bought
His pennyworth of wonder,
                              So they thought,
Till all at once Fitzwarren's daughter cried
'Father, you have forgot poor Whittington!'
' 'Snails,' laughed the rosy marchaunt, ' but that's true!
Fetch Whittington! The lad must stake his groat!
'Twill bring us luck!'
                              'Whittington! Whittington!'
Down the dark stair, like a gold-headed bird,
Fluttered sweet Alice. 'Whittington! Richard! Quick!
Quick with your groat now for the *Unicorn!'*

' A groat!' cried Whittington, standing there aghast,
With brown bare arms, still coloured by the sun,

Among his pots and pans. 'Where should I find
A groat? I staked my last groat in a cat!'
—'What! Have you nothing? Nothing but a cat?
Then stake the cat,' she said; and the quick fire
That in a woman's mind out-runs the thought
Of man, lit her grey eyes.

                    Whittington laughed
And opened the cellar-door. Out sailed his wealth,
Waving its tail, purring, and rubbing its head
Now on his boots, now on the dainty shoe
Of Alice, who straightway, deaf to his laughing prayers,
Caught up the cat, whispered it, hugged it close,
Against its grey fur leaned her glowing cheek,
And carried it off in triumph.

                       Red Rose Lane
Echoed with laughter as, with amber eyes
Blinking, the grey cat in a seaman's arms
Went to the wharf. 'Ay, but we need a cat,'
The captain said. So, when the painted ship
Sailed through a golden sunrise down the Thames,
A grey tail waved upon the misty poop,
And Whittington had his venture on the seas.

It was a nine days' jest, and soon forgot.
But, all that year,— ah, sirs, ye know the world,
For all the foolish boasting of the proud,
Looks not beneath the coat of Taunton serge
For Gules and Azure. A prince that comes in rags
To clean your shoes and, out of his own pride,
Waits for the world to paint his shield again
Must wait for ever and a day.

[188]

                                  The world
Is a great hypocrite, hypocrite most of all
When thus it boasts its purple pride of race,
Then with eyes blind to all but pride of place
Tramples the scullion's heraldry underfoot,
Nay, never sees it, never dreams of it,
Content to know that, here and now, his coat
Is greasy . . .
                        So did Whittington find at last
Such nearness was most distant; that to see her,
Talk with her, serve her thus, was but to lose
True sight, true hearing. He must save his life
By losing it; forsake, to win, his love;
Go out into the world to bring her home.
It was but labour to clean the shoes,
And turn the jack, and scour the dripping-pan.
For every scolding blown about her ears
The cook's great ladle fell upon the head
Of Whittington; who, beneath her rule, became
The scullery's general scapegoat. It was he
That burned the pie-crust, drank the hippocras,
Dinted the silver beaker. . . .
                              Many a month
He chafed, till his resolve took sudden shape
And, out of the dark house at the peep of day,
Shouldering bundle and stick again, he stole
To seek his freedom, and to shake the dust
Of London from his shoes. . . .
                              You know the stone
On Highgate, where he sate awhile to rest,
With aching heart, and thought 'I shall not see

Her face again.' There, as the coloured dawn
Over the sleeping City slowly bloomed,
A small black battered ship with tattered sails
Blurring the burnished glamour of the Thames
Crept, side-long to a wharf.

　　　　　　　　　Then, all at once,
The London bells rang out a welcome home;
And, over them all, tossing the tenor on high,
The Bell of Bow, a sun among the stars,
Flooded the morning air with this refrain:—

'Turn again, Whittington! Turn again, Whittington!
　Flos Mercatorum, thy ship hath come home!
Trailing from her cross-trees the crimson of the sunrise,
　Dragging all the glory of the sunset thro' the foam.
　　　　Turn again, Whittington,
　　　　Turn again, Whittington,
　　　　　Lord Mayor of London!

Turn again, Whittington! When thy hope was darkest,
　Far beyond the sky-line a ship sailed for thee.
Flos Mercatorum, O, when thy faith was blindest,
　Even then thy sails were set beyond the Ocean-sea.'

So he heard and heeded us, and turned again to London,
　Stick and bundle on his back, he turned to *Red Rose Lane,*
Hardly hearing as he went the chatter of the prentices,—
　*What d'ye lack, and what d'ye lack, and what d'ye lack
　　again?*

[190]

Back into the scullery, before the cook had missed him,
   Early in the morning his labours he began:
Once again to clean the shoes and clatter with the water-
      pail,
   Once again to scrub the jack and scour the dripping-pan.

All the bells of London were pealing as he laboured.
   Wildly beat his heart, and his blood began to race.
Then — there came a light step and, suddenly, beside him
   Stood his lady Alice, with a light upon her face.

'Quick,' she said, 'O, quick,' she said, 'they want you,
      Richard Whittington!'
   'Quick,' she said; and, while she spoke, her lighted eyes
      betrayed
All that she had hidden long, and all she still would hide
      from him.
   So — he turned and followed her, his green-gowned maid.

   .   .   .   .

There, in a broad dark oaken-panelled room
Rich with black carvings and great gleaming cups
Of silver, sirs, and massy halpace built
Half over *Red Rose Lane,* Fitzwarren sat;
And, at his side, O, like an old romance
That suddenly comes true and fills the world
With April colours, two bronzed seamen stood,
Tattered and scarred, and stained with sun and brine.
'*Flos Mercatorum,*' Hugh Fitzwarren cried,
Holding both hands out to the pale-faced boy,
'The prentice wins the prize! Why, Whittington,
Thy cat hath caught the biggest mouse of all!'

And, on to the table, tilting a heavy sack,
One of the seamen poured a glittering stream
Of rubies, emeralds, opals, amethysts,
That turned the room to an Aladdin's cave,
Or magic goblet brimmed with dusky wine
Where clustering rainbow-coloured bubbles clung
And sparkled, in the halls of Prester John.

' And that,' said Hugh Fitzwarren, ' is the price
Paid for your cat in Barbary, by a King
Whose house was rich in gems, but sorely plagued
With rats and mice.   Gather it up, my lad,
And praise your master for his honesty;
For, though my cargo prospered, yours out-shines
The best of it.   Take it, my lad, and go;
You're a rich man; and, if you use it well,
Riches will make you richer, and the world
Will prosper in your own prosperity.
The miser, like the cold and barren moon,
Shines with a fruitless light.   The spendthrift fool
Flits like a Jack-o-Lent over quags and fens;
But he that's wisely rich gathers his gold
Into a fruitful and unwasting sun
That spends its glory on a thousand fields
And blesses all the world.   Take it and go.'

Blankly, as in a dream, Whittington stared.
' How should I take it, sir?   The ship was yours,
And . . .'
                          ' Ay, the ship was mine; but in that ship
Your stake was richer than we knew.   'Tis yours.'

'Then,' answered Whittington, 'if this wealth be mine,
Who but an hour ago was all so poor,
I know one way to make me richer still.'
He gathered up the glittering sack of gems,
Turned to the halpace, where his green-gowned maid
Stood in the glory of the coloured panes.
He thrust the splendid load into her arms,
Muttering —'Take it, lady! Let me be poor!
But rich, at least, in that you not despise
The waif you saved.'

                —'Despise you, Whittington?'—
'O, no, not in the sight of God! But I
Grow tired of waiting for the Judgment Day!
I am but a man. I am a scullion now;
But I would like, only for half an hour,
To stand upright and say "I am a king!"
Take it!'

        And, as they stood, a little apart,
Their eyes were married in one swift level look,
Silent, but all that souls could say was said.

   •   •   •   •   •   •

                       And
'I know a way,' said the Bell of St. Martin's.
  'Tell it, and be quick,' laughed the prentices below!
'Whittington shall marry her, marry her, marry her!
  Peal for a wedding,' said the big Bell of Bow.

He shall take a kingdom up, and cast it on the sea again;
  He shall have his caravels to traffic for him now;
He shall see his royal sails rolling up from Araby,
  And the crest — a honey-bee — golden at the prow.

Whittington! Whittington! The world is all a fairy tale!—
Even so we sang for him.— But O, the tale is true!
Whittington he married her, and on his merry marriage-day,
  O, we sang, we sang for him, like lavrocks in the blue.

Far away from London, these happy prentice lovers
  Wandered through the summer to his western home again,
Down by deep Dorset to the wooded isle of Purbeck,
  Round to little Kimmeridge, by many a lover's lane.

There did they abide as in a dove-cote hidden
  Deep in happy woods till the bells of duty rang;
Then they rode the way he went, a barefoot boy to London,
  Round by Hampshire forest-roads, but as they rode he
    sang:—

Kimmeridge in Dorset is the happiest of places!
  All the little homesteads are thatched with beauty there!
All the old ploughmen, there, have happy smiling faces,
  Christmas roses in their cheeks, and crowns of silver hair.

Blue as are the eggs in the nest of the hedge-sparrow,
  Gleam the little rooms in the homestead that I know:
Death, I think, has lost the way to Kimmeridge in Dorset;
  Sorrow never knew it, or forgot it, long ago!

Kimmeridge in Dorset, Kimmeridge in Dorset,
  Though I may not see you more thro' all the years to be,
Yet will I remember the little happy homestead
  Hidden in that Paradise where God was good to me.

   .   .   .   .   .   .

So they turned to London, and with mind and soul he laboured,
  Flos Mercatorum, for the mighty years to be,
Fashioning, for profit — to the years that should forget him!—
  This, our sacred City that must shine upon the sea.

London was a City when the Poulters ruled the Poultry!
  Rosaries of prayer were hung in Paternoster Row,
Gutter Lane was Guthrun's, then; and, bright with painted missal-books,
  Ave Mary Corner, sirs, was fairer than ye know.

London was mighty when her marchaunts loved their merchandise,
  Bales of Eastern magic that empurpled wharf and quay:
London was mighty when her booths were a dream-market,
  Loaded with the colours of the sunset and the sea.

There, in all their glory, with the Virgin on their bannerols,
  Glory out of Genoa, the Mercers might be seen,
Walking to their Company of Marchaunt Adventurers; —
  Gallantly they jetted it in scarlet and in green.

There, in all the glory of the lordly Linen Armourers,
  Walked the Marchaunt Taylors with the Pilgrim of their trade,
Fresh from adventuring in Italy and Flanders,
  Flos Mercatorum, for a green-gowned maid.

Flos Mercatorum! Can a good thing come of Nazareth?
  High above the darkness, where our duller senses drown,

[195]

Lifts the splendid Vision of a City, built on merchandise,
　　Fairer than that City of Light that wore the violet crown,

Lifts the sacred vision of a far-resplendent City,
　　Flashing, like the heart of heaven, its messages afar,
Trafficking, as God Himself, through all His interchanging
　　　　worlds,
　　Holding up the scales of law, weighing star by star,

Stern as Justice, in one hand the sword of Truth and Right-
　　　　eousness;
　　Blind as Justice, in one hand the everlasting scales,
Lifts the sacred Vision of that City from the darkness,
　　Whence the thoughts of men break out, like blossoms, or
　　　　like sails!

Ordered and harmonious, a City built to music,
　　Lifting, out of chaos, the shining towers of law,—
Ay, a sacred City, and a City built of merchandise,
　　Flos Mercatorum, was the City that he saw.

And by that light," quoth Clopton, " did he keep
His promise.　He was rich; but in his will
He wrote those words which should be blazed with gold
In London's *Liber Albus:*—

　　　　　　　　The desire
　　And busy intention of a man, devout
　　And wise, should be to fore-cast and secure
　　The state and end of this short life with deeds
　　Of mercy and pity, especially to provide
　　　　　　　　[196]

> For those whom poverty insulteth; those
> To whom the power of labouring for the needs
> Of life, is interdicted.

         He became
The Father of the City. Felons died
Of fever in old Newgate. He rebuilt
The prison. London sickened from the lack
Of water, and he made fresh fountains flow.
He heard the cry of suffering and disease,
And built the stately hospital that still
Shines like an angel's lanthorn through the night,
The stately halls of St. Bartholomew.
He saw men wrapt in ignorance, and he raised
Schools, colleges, and libraries. He heard
The cry of the old and weary, and he built
Houses of refuge.
      Even so he kept
His prentice vows of Duty, Industry,
Obedience, words contemned of every fool
Who shrinks from law; yet were those ancient vows
The adamantine pillars of the State.
Let all who play their Samson be well warned
That Samsons perish, too!
        His monument
Is London!"
     " Ay," quoth Dekker, " and he deserves
Well of the Mermaid Inn for one good law,
Rightly enforced. He pilloried that rogue
Will Horold, who in Whittington's third year
Of office, as Lord Mayor, placed certain gums

And spices in great casks, and filled them up
With feeble Spanish wine, to have the taste
And smell of Romeney,— Malmsey!"

                        "Honest wine,
Indeed," replied the Clerk, "concerns the State,
That solemn structure touched with light from heaven,
Which he, our merchant, helped to build on earth.
And, while he laboured for it, all things else
Were added unto him, until the bells
More than fulfilled their prophecy.

                        One great eve,
Fair Alice, leaning from her casement, saw
Another Watch, and mightier than the first,
Billowing past the newly painted doors
Of Whittington Palace — so men called his house
In Hart Street, fifteen yards from old Mark Lane,—
A thousand burganets and halberdiers,
A thousand archers in their white silk coats,
A thousand mounted men in ringing mail,
A thousand sworded henchmen; then, his Guild,
Advancing, on their splendid bannerols
The Virgin, glorious in gold; and then,
Flos Mercatorum, on his great stirring steed
Whittington! On that night he made a feast
For London and the King. His feasting hall
Gleamed like the magic cave that Prester John
Wrought out of one huge opal. East and West
Lavished their wealth on that great Citizen
Who, when the King from Agincourt returned
Victorious, but with empty coffers, lent
Three times the ransom of an Emperor

To fill them — on the royal bond, and said
When the King questioned him of how and whence,
'I am the steward of your City, sire!
There is a sea, and who shall drain it dry?'
  Over the roasted swans and peacock pies,
The minstrels in the great black gallery tuned
All hearts to mirth, until it seemed their cups
Were brimmed with dawn and sunset, and they drank
The wine of gods. Lord of a hundred ships,
Under the feet of England, Whittington flung
The purple of the seas. And when the Queen,
Catharine, wondered at the costly woods
That burned upon his hearth, the Marchaunt rose,
He drew the great sealed parchments from his breast,
The bonds the King had given him on his loans,
Loans that might drain the Mediterranean dry.
'They call us hucksters, madam, we that love
Our City,' and, into the red-hot heart of the fire,
He tossed the bonds of sixty thousand pounds.
'The fire burns low,' said Richard Whittington.
Then, overhead, the minstrels plucked their strings;
And, over the clash of wine-cups, rose a song
That made the old timbers of their feasting-hall
Shake, as a galleon shakes in a gale of wind,
When she rolls glorying through the Ocean-sea:—

Marchaunt Adventurers, O, what shall it profit you
  Thus to seek your kingdom in the dream-destroying sun?
Ask us why the hawthorn brightens on the sky-line:
  Even so our sails break out when Spring is well begun!

Flos Mercatorum! Blossom wide, ye sails of England,
   Hasten ye the kingdom, now the bitter days are done!
Ay, for we be members, one of another,
   ' Each for all and all for each,' quoth Richard Whittington!

Chorus :—   Marchaunt Adventurers,
                 Marchaunt Adventurers,
   Marchaunt Adventurers, the Spring is well begun!
Break, break out on every sea, O, fair white sails of England!
   ' Each for all, and all for each,' quoth Richard Whitting-
      ton.

Marchaunt Adventurers, O what 'ull ye bring home again?
   Woonders and works and the thunder of the sea!
Whom will ye traffic with? The King of the sunset!—
   What shall be your pilot, then?— A wind from Galilee!
— Nay, but ye be marchaunts, will ye come back empty-
      handed?—
   Ay, we be marchaunts, though our gain we ne'er shall see!
Cast we now our bread upon the waste wild waters;
   After many days it shall return with usury.

Chorus :—   Marchaunt Adventurers,
                 Marchaunt Adventurers,
   What shall be your profit in the mighty days to be?
Englande! Englande! Englande! Englande!
   Glory everlasting and the lordship of the sea.

What need to tell you, sirs, how Whittington
Remembered? Night and morning, as he knelt
In those old days, O, like two children still,

Whittington and his Alice bowed their heads
Together, praying.
                From such simple hearts,
O never doubt it, though the whole world doubt
The God that made it, came the steadfast strength
Of England, all that once was her strong soul,
The soul that laughed and shook away defeat
As her strong cliffs hurl back the streaming seas.
Sirs, in his old age Whittington returned,
And stood with Alice, by the silent tomb
In little Pauntley church.
                There, to his Arms,
The Gules and Azure, and the Lion's Head
So proudly blazoned on the painted panes;
(O, sirs, the simple wistfulness of it
Might move hard hearts to laughter, but I think
Tears tremble through it, for the Mermaid Inn)
He added his new crest, the hard-won sign
And lowly prize of his own industry,
The Honey-bee.   And, far away, the bells
Peal softly from the pure white City of God:—

        Ut fragrans nardus   •
        Fama fuit iste Ricardus.

With folded hands he waits the Judgment, now.
Slowly our dark bells toll across the world,
For him who waits the reckoning, his accompt
Secure, his conscience clear, his ledger spread
A *Liber Albus* flooded with pure light.

> *Flos Mercatorum,*
> *Fundator presbyterorum, . . .*

Slowly the dark bells toll for him who asks
No more of men, but that they may sometimes
Pray for the souls of Richard Whittington,
Alice, his wife, and (as themselves of old
Had prayed) the father and mother of each of them.
Slowly the great notes fall and float away:—

> *Omnibus exemplum*
> *Barathrum vincendo morosum*
> *Condidit hoc templum . . .*
> *Pauperibus pater . . . . .*
> *Finiit ipse dies*
> *Sis sibi Christe quies. Amen."*

IX
RALEIGH

RALEIGH

BEN was our only guest that day. His tribe
    Had flown to their new shrine — the Apollo Room,
To which, though they enscrolled his golden verse
Above their doors like some great-fruited vine,
Ben still preferred our *Mermaid,* and to smoke
Alone in his old nook; perhaps to hear
The voices of the dead,
The voices of his old companions,
Hovering near him,— Will and Kit and Rob.

" Our Ocean-shepherd from the Main-deep sea,
Raleigh," he muttered, as I brimmed his cup,
" Last of the men that broke the fleets of Spain,
'Twas not enough to cage him, sixteen years,
Rotting his heart out in the Bloody Tower,
But they must fling him forth in his old age
To hunt for El Dorado. Then, mine host,
Because his poor old ship *The Destiny*
Smashes the Spaniard, but comes tottering home
Without the Spanish gold, our gracious king,
To please a catamite,
Sends the old lion back to the Tower again.
The friends of Spain will send him to the block

[205]

This time. That male Salome, Buckingham,
Is dancing for his head. Raleigh is doomed."
A shadow stood in the doorway. We looked up;
And there, but O, how changed, how worn and grey,
Sir Walter Raleigh, like a hunted thing,
Stared at us.
     "Ben," he said, and glanced behind him.
Ben took a step towards him.
        "O, my God,
Ben," whispered the old man in a husky voice,
Half timorous and half cunning, so unlike
His old heroic self that one might weep
To hear it, "Ben, I have given them all the slip!
I may be followed. Can you hide me here
Till it grows dark?"
Ben drew him quickly in, and motioned me
To lock the door. "Till it grows dark," he cried,
"My God, that you should ask it!"
         "Do not think,
Do not believe that I am quite disgraced,"
The old man faltered, "for they'll say it, Ben;
And when my boy grows up, they'll tell him, too,
His father was a coward. I do cling
To life for many reasons, not from fear
Of death. No, Ben, I can disdain that still;
But — there's my boy!"
       Then all his face went blind.
He dropt upon Ben's shoulder and sobbed outright,
"They are trying to break my pride, to break my pride!"
The window darkened, and I saw a face
Blurring the panes. Ben gripped the old man's arm,

SIR WALTER RALEIGH

From a Painting in the Collection of the Duchess of Dorset

And led him gently to a room within,
Out of the way of guests.

                   "Your pride," he said,
"That is the pride of England!"

                           At that name —
England! —
As at a signal-gun, heard in the night
Far out at sea, the weather and world-worn man,
That once was Raleigh, lifted up his head.
Old age and weakness, weariness and fear
Fell from him like a cloak. He stood erect.
His eager eyes, full of great sea-washed dawns,
Burned for a moment with immortal youth,
While tears blurred mine to see him.

                      "You do think
That England will remember? You do think it?"
He asked with a great light upon his face.
Ben bowed his head in silence.

    .   .   .   .

                     "I have wronged
My cause by this," said Raleigh. "Well they know it
Who left this way for me. I have flung myself
Like a blind moth into this deadly light
Of freedom. Now, at the eleventh hour,
Is it too late? I might return and —

                       "No!
Not now!" Ben interrupted. "I'd have said
Laugh at the headsman sixteen years ago,
When England was awake. She will awake
Again. But now, while our most gracious king,
Who hates tobacco, dedicates his prayers

To Buckingham —
This is no land for men that, under God,
Shattered the Fleet Invincible."
                                        A knock
Startled us, at the outer door. "My friend
Stukeley," said Raleigh, "if I know his hand.
He has a ketch will carry me to France,
Waiting at Tilbury."
                        I let him in,—
A lean and stealthy fellow, Sir Lewis Stukeley,—
I liked him little. He thought much of his health,
More of his money bags, and most of all
On how to run with all men all at once
For his own profit. At the *Mermaid Inn*
Men disagreed in friendship and in truth;
But he agreed with all men, and his life
Was one soft quag of falsehood. Fugitives
Must use false keys, I thought; and there was hope
For Raleigh if such a man would walk one mile
To serve him now. Yet my throat moved to see him
Usurping, with one hand on Raleigh's arm,
A kind of ownership. *"Lend me ten pounds,"*
Were the first words he breathed in the old man's ear,
And Raleigh slipped his purse into his hand.

        .   .   .   .

Just over Bread Street hung the bruised white moon
When they crept out. Sir Lewis Stukeley's watch-dog,
A derelict bo'sun, with a mulberry face,
Met them outside. "The coast quite clear, eh, Hart?"
Said Stukeley. "Ah, that's good. Lead on, then, quick."
And there, framed in the cruddle of moonlit clouds

That ended the steep street, dark on its light,
And standing on those glistening cobble-stones
Just where they turned to silver, Raleigh looked back
Before he turned the corner. He stood there.
A figure like foot-feathered Mercury,
Tall, straight and splendid, waving his plumed hat
To Ben, and taking his last look, I felt,
Upon our *Mermaid Tavern*. As he paused,
His long fantastic shadow swayed and swept
Against our feet. Then, like a shadow, he passed.

"It is not right," said Ben, "it is not right.
Why did they give the old man so much grace?
Witness and evidence are what they lack.
Would you trust Stukeley — not to draw him out?
Raleigh was always rash. A phrase or two
Will turn their murderous axe into a sword
Of righteousness —
                    Why, come to think of it,
Blackfriar's Wharf, last night, I landed there,
And — no, by God! — Raleigh is not himself,
The tide will never serve beyond Gravesend.
It is a trap! Come on! We'll follow them!
Quick! To the river side!"—
                            We reached the wharf
Only to see their wherry, a small black cloud
Dwindling far down that running silver road.
Ben touched my arm.
"Look there," he said, pointing up stream.
                                        The moon
Glanced on a cluster of pikes, like silver thorns,

[209]

Three hundred yards away, a little troop
Of weaponed men, embarking hurriedly.
Their great black wherry clumsily swung about,
Then, with twelve oars for legs, came striding down,
An armoured beetle on the glittering trail
Of some small victim.

                    Just below our wharf
A little dinghy waddled.
Ben cut the painter, and without one word
Drew her up crackling thro' the lapping water,
Motioned me to the tiller, thrust her off,
And, pulling with one oar, backing with the other,
Swirled her round and down, hard on the track
Of Raleigh. Ben was an old man now, but tough,
O tough as a buccaneer. We distanced them.
His oar blades drove the silver boiling back.
By Broken Wharf the beetle was a speck.
It dwindled by Queen Hythe and the Three Cranes.
By Bellyn's Gate we had left it, out of sight.
By Custom House and Galley Keye we shot
Thro' silver all the way, without one glimpse
Of Raleigh. Then a dreadful shadow fell
And over us the Tower of London rose
Like ebony; and, on the glittering reach
Beyond it, I could see the small black cloud
That carried the great old seaman slowly down
Between the dark shores whence in happier years
The throng had cheered his golden galleons out,
And watched his proud sails filling for Cathay.
There, as through lead, we dragged by Traitor's Gate,
There, in the darkness, under the Bloody Tower,

There, on the very verge of victory,
Ben gasped and dropped his oars.
"Take one and row," he said, "my arms are numbed.
We'll overtake him yet!"   I clambered past him,
And took the bow oar.

                  Once, as the pace flagged,
Over his shoulder he turned his great scarred face
And snarled, with a trickle of blood on his coarse lips,
"Hard!"—
And blood and fire ran through my veins again,
For half a minute more.

                  Yet we fell back.
Our course was crookéd now.   And suddenly
A grim black speck began to grow behind us,
Grow like the threat of death upon old age.
Then, thickening, blackening, sharpening, foaming, swept
Up the bright line of bubbles in our wake,
That armoured wherry, with its long twelve oars
All well together now.

                "Too late," gasped Ben,
His ash-grey face uplifted to the moon,
One quivering hand upon the thwart behind him,
A moment. Then he bowed over his knees
Coughing.   "But we'll delay them.   We'll be drunk,
And hold the catch-polls up!"

                  We drifted down
Before them, broadside on.   They sheered aside.
Then, feigning a clumsy stroke, Ben drove our craft
As they drew level, right in among their blades.
There was a shout, an oath.   They thrust us off;
And then we swung our nose against their bows

And pulled them round with every well-meant stroke.
A full half minute, ere they won quite free,
Cursing us for a pair of drunken fools.

We drifted down behind them.
                              " There's no doubt,"
Said Ben, " the headsman waits behind all this
For Raleigh. This is a play to cheat the soul
Of England, teach the people to applaud
The red fifth act."
Without another word we drifted down
For centuries it seemed, until we came
To Greenwich.
Then up the long white burnished reach there crept
Like little sooty clouds the two black boats
To meet us.
              " He is in the trap," said Ben,
" And does not know it yet. See, where he sits
By Stukeley as by a friend."
                              Long after this,
We heard how Raleigh, simply as a child,
Seeing the tide would never serve him now,
And they must turn, had taken from his neck
Some trinkets that he wore. " Keep them," he said
To Stukeley, " in remembrance of this night."

He had no doubts of Stukeley when he saw
The wherry, close beside them. He but wrapped
His cloak a little closer round his face.
Our boat rocked in their wash when Stukeley dropped
The mask. We saw him give the sign, and heard

His   high-pitched   quavering   voice — "IN   THE   KING'S
    NAME!"
Raleigh rose to his feet.   "I am under arrest?"
He said, like a dazed man.
                  And Stukeley laughed.
Then, as he bore himself to the grim end,
All doubt being over, the old sea-king stood
Among those glittering points, a king indeed.
The black boats rocked.   We heard his level voice,
"Sir Lewis, these actions never will turn out
To your good credit."   Across the moonlit Thames
It rang contemptuously, cold as cold steel,
And passionless as the judgment that ends all.

     .   .   .   .

Some three months later, Raleigh's widow came
To lodge a se'nnight at the Mermaid Inn.
His house in Bread Street was no more her own,
But in the hands of Stukeley, who had reaped
A pretty harvest. . . .
She kept close to her room, and that same night,
Being ill and with some fever, sent her maid
To fetch the apothecary from Friday Street,
Old "Galen" as the Mermaid christened him.
At that same moment, as the maid went out,
Stukeley came in.   He met her at the door;
And, chucking her under the chin, gave her a letter.
"Take this up to your mistress.   It concerns
Her property," he said.   "Say that I wait,
And would be glad to speak with her."

         The wench
Looked pertly in his face, and tripped upstairs.
I scarce could trust my hands.
        "Sir Lewis," I said,
"This is no time to trouble her. She is ill."
"Let her decide," he answered, with a sneer.
Before I found another word to say
The maid tripped down again. I scarce believed
My senses, when she beckoned him up the stair.
Shaking from head to foot, I blocked the way.
"Property!" Could the crux of mine and thine
Bring widow and murderer into one small room?
"Sir Lewis," I said, "she is ill. It is not right!
She never would consent."
       He sneered again,
"You are her doctor? Out of the way, old fool!
She has decided!"
      "Go," I said to the maid,
"Fetch the apothecary. Let it rest
With him!"
     She tossed her head. Her quick eyes glanced,
Showing the white, like the eyes of a vicious mare.
She laughed at Stukeley, loitered, then obeyed.

And so we waited, till the wench returned,
With Galen at her heels. His wholesome face,
Russet and wrinkled like an apple, peered
Shrewdly at Stukeley, twinkled once at me,
And passed in silence, leaving a whiff of herbs
Behind him on the stair.

Five minutes later
To my amazement, that same wholesome face
Leaned from the lighted door above, and called
" Sir Lewis Stukeley ! "

Sir Judas hastened up.
The apothecary followed him within.
The door shut. I was left there in the dark
Bewildered; for my heart was hot with thoughts
Of those last months. Our Summer's Nightingale,
Our Ocean-Shepherd from the Main-deep Sea,
The Founder of our Mermaid Fellowship,
Was this his guerdon — at the Mermaid Inn?
Was this that maid-of-honour whose romance
With Raleigh, once, had been a kingdom's talk?
Could Bess Throckmorton slight his memory thus?
" It is not right," I said, " it is not right.
She wrongs him deeply."

I leaned against the porch
Staring into the night. A ghostly ray
Above me, from her window, bridged the street,
And rested on the goldsmith's painted sign
Opposite.

I could hear the muffled voice.
Of Stukeley overhead, persuasive, bland;
And then, her own, cooing, soft as a dove
Calling her mate from Eden cedar-boughs,
Flowed on and on; and then — all my flesh crept
At something worse than either, a long space
Of silence that stretched threatening and cold,
Cold as a dagger-point pricking the skin
Over my heart.

[215]

                              Then came a stifled cry,
A crashing door, a footstep on the stair
Blundering like a drunkard's, heavily down;
And with his gasping face one tragic mask
Of horror,— may God help me to forget
Some day the frozen awful eyes of one
Who, fearing neither hell nor heaven, has met
That ultimate weapon of the gods, the face
And serpent-tresses that turn flesh to stone —
Stukeley stumbled, groping his way out,
Blindly, past me, into the sheltering night.

    .   .   .   .

It was the last night of another year
Before I understood what punishment
Had overtaken Stukeley. Ben, and Brome,—
Ben's ancient servant, but turned poet now —
Sat by the fire with the old apothecary
To see the New Year in.
                              The starry night
Had drawn me to the door. Could it be true
That our poor earth no longer was the hub
Of those white wheeling orbs? I scarce believed
The strange new dreams; but I had seen the veils
Rent from vast oceans and huge continents,
Till what was once our comfortable fire,
Our cosy tavern, and our earthly home
With heaven beyond the next turn in the road,
All the resplendent fabric of our world
Shrank to a glow-worm, lighting up one leaf
In one small forest, in one little land,
Among those wild infinitudes of God.

A tattered wastrel wandered down the street,
Clad in a seaman's jersey, staring hard
At every sign. Beneath our own, the light
Fell on his red carbuncled face. I knew him —
The bo'sun, Hart.

               He pointed to our sign
And leered at me. "That's her," he said, "no doubt,
The sea-witch with the shiny mackerel tail
Swishing in wine. That's what Sir Lewis meant.
He called it blood. Blood is his craze, you see.
This is the Mermaid Tavern, sir, no doubt?"
I nodded. "Ah, I thought as much," he said.
"Well — happen this is worth a cup of ale."
He thrust his hand under his jersey and lugged
A greasy letter out. It was inscribed
THE APOTHECARY AT THE MERMAID TAVERN.
I led him in. "I knew it, sir," he said,
While Galen broke the seal. "Soon as I saw
That sweet young naked wench curling her tail
In those red waves.— The old man called it blood.
Blood is his craze, you see.— But you can tell
'Tis wine, sir, by the foam. Malmsey, no doubt.
And that sweet wench to make you smack your lips
Like oysters, with her slippery tail and all!
Why, sir, no doubt, this was the Mermaid Inn."

"But this," said Galen, lifting his grave face
To Ben, "this letter is from all that's left
Of Stukeley. The good host, there, thinks I wronged
Your Ocean-shepherd's memory. From this letter,
I think I helped to avenge him. Do not wrong

His widow, even in thought. She loved him dearly.
You know she keeps his poor grey severed head
Embalmed; and so will keep it till she dies;
Weeps over it alone. I have heard such things
In wild Italian tales. But *this* was true.
Had I refused to let her speak with Stukeley
I feared she would go mad. This letter proves
That I — and she perhaps — were instruments,
Of some more terrible chirurgery
Than either knew."

                " Ah, when I saw your sign,"
The bo'sun interjected, " I'd no doubt
That letter was well worth a cup of ale."

  " Go — paint your bows with hell-fire somewhere else
Not at this inn," said Ben, tossing the rogue
A good French crown. " Pickle yourself in hell."
And Hart lurched out into the night again,
Muttering " Thank you, sirs. 'Twas worth all that.
No doubt at all."

              " There are some men," said Galen,
Spreading the letter out on his plump knees,
" Will heap up wrong on wrong; and, at the last,
Wonder because the world will not forget
Just when it suits them, cancel all they owe,
And, like a mother, hold its arms out wide
At their first cry. And, sirs, I do believe
That Stukeley, on that night, had some such wish
To reconcile himself. What else had passed
Between the widow and himself I know not;
But she had lured him on until he thought
That words and smiles, perhaps a tear or two,

Might make the widow take the murderer's hand
In friendship, since it might advantage both.
Indeed, he came prepared for even more.
Villains are always fools.   A wicked act,
What is it but a false move in the game,
A blind man's blunder, a deaf man's reply,
The wrong drug taken in the dead of night?
I always pity villains.

                    I mistook
The avenger for the victim.   There she lay
Panting, that night, her eyes like summer stars.
Her pale gold hair upon the pillows tossed
Dishevelled, while the fever in her face
Brought back the lost wild roses of her youth
For half an hour.   Against a breast as pure
And smooth as any maid's, her soft arms pressed
A bundle wrapped in a white embroidered cloth.
She crooned over it as a mother croons
Over her suckling child.   I stood beside her.
— That was her wish, and mine, while Stukeley stayed.—
And, over against me, on the other side,
Stood Stukeley, gnawing his nether lip to find
She could not, or she would not, speak one word
In answer to his letter.

                         " Lady Raleigh,
You wrong me, and you wrong yourself," he cried,
" To play like a green girl when great affairs
Are laid before you.   Let me speak with you
Alone."

            " But I am all alone," she said,
" Far more alone than I have ever been

In all my life before. This is my doctor.
He must not leave me."

                    Then she lured him on,
Played on his brain as a musician plays
Upon the lute.

                  " Forgive me, dear Sir Lewis,
If I am grown too gay for widowhood.
But I have pondered for a long, long time
On all these matters. I know the world was right;
And Spain was right, Sir Lewis. Yes, and you,
You too, were right; and my poor husband wrong.
You see I knew his mind so very well.
I knew his every gesture, every smile.
I lived with him. I think I died with him.
It is a strange thing, marriage. For my soul
(As if myself were present in this flesh)
Beside him, slept in his grey prison-cell
On that last dreadful dawn. I heard the throng
Murmuring round the scaffold far away;
And, with the smell of saw-dust in my nostrils,
I woke, bewildered as himself, to see
That tall black-cassocked figure by his bed.
I heard the words that made him understand:
The Body of our Lord — take and eat this!
I rolled the small sour flakes beneath my tongue
With him. I caught, with him, the gleam of tears,
Far off, on some strange face of sickly dread.
The Blood — and the cold cup was in my hand,
Cold as an axe-heft washed with waterish red.
I heard his last poor cry to wife and child.—
Could any that heard forget it ? — *My true God,*

[220]

Hold you both in His arms, both in His arms.
And then — that last poor wish, a thing to raise
A smile in some. I have smiled at it myself
A thousand times.

     ' Give me my pipe,' he said,
' My old Winchester clay, with the long stem,
And half an hour alone. The crowd can wait.
They have not waited half so long as I.'
And then, O then, I know what soft blue clouds,
What wavering rings, fragrant ascending wreaths
Melted his prison walls to a summer haze,
Through which I think he saw the little port
Of Budleigh Salterton, like a sea-bird's nest
Among the Devon cliffs — the tarry quay
Whence in his boyhood he had flung a line
For bass or whiting-pollock. I remembered
(Had he not told me, on some summer night,
His arm about my neck, kissing my hair)
He used to sit there, gazing out to sea;
Fish, and for what? Not all for what he caught
And handled; but for rainbow-coloured things,
The water-drops that jewelled his thin line,
Flotsam and jetsam of the sunset-clouds;
While the green water, gurgling through the piles,
Heaving and sinking, helped him to believe
The fast-bound quay a galleon plunging out
Superbly for Cathay. There would he sit
Listening, a radiant boy, child of the sea,
Listening to some old seaman's glowing tales,
His grey eyes rich with pictures —

[221]

                              Then he saw,
And I with him, that gathering in the West,
To break the Fleet Invincible. O, I heard
The trumpets and the neighings and the drums.
I watched the beacons on a hundred hills.
I drank that wine of battle from *his* cup,
And gloried in it, lying against his heart.
I sailed with him and saw the unknown worlds!
The slender ivory towers of old Cathay
Rose for us over lilac-coloured seas
That crumbled a sky-blue foam on long shores
Of shining sand, shores of so clear a glass
They drew the sunset-clouds into their bosom
And hung that City of Vision in mid-air
Girdling it round, as with a moat of sky,
Hopelessly beautiful. O, yet I heard,
Heard from his blazoned poops the trumpeters
Blowing proud calls, while overhead the flag
Of England floated from white towers of sail —
And yet, and yet, I knew that he was wrong,
And soon he knew it, too.

                         I saw the cloud
Of doubt assail him, in the Bloody Tower,
When, being withheld from sailing the high seas
For sixteen years, he spread a prouder sail,
Took up his pen, and, walled about with stone,
Began to write — his *History of the World*.
And emperors came like Lazarus from the grave
To wear his purple.   And the night disgorged
Its empires, till, O, like the swirl of dust
Around their marching legions, that dim cloud

Of doubt closed round him. Was there any man
So sure of heart and brain as to record
The simple truth of things himself had seen?
Then who could plumb that night? The work broke off!
He knew that he was wrong. I knew it, too!
Once more that stately structure of his dreams
Melted like mist. His eagles perished like clouds.
Death wound a thin horn through the centuries.
The grave resumed his forlorn emperors.
His empires crumbled back to a little ash
Knocked from his pipe.—
He dropped his pen in homage to the truth.
The truth? *O, eloquent, just and mighty Death!*

Then, when he forged, out of one golden thought,
A key to open his prison; when the king
Released him for a tale of faërie gold
Under the tropic palms; when those grey walls
Melted before his passion; do you think
The gold that lured the king was quite the same
As that which Raleigh saw? You know the song:
            ' Say to the King,' quoth Raleigh,
               ' I have a tale to tell him;
                  Wealth beyond derision,
                     Veils to lift from the sky,
               Seas to sail for England,
                  And a little dream to sell him,
                     Gold, the gold of a vision
                        That angels cannot buy.'

Ah, no! For all the beauty and the pride,

Raleigh was wrong; but not so wrong, I think,
As those for whom his kingdoms oversea
Meant only glittering dust. The fight he waged
Was not with them. They never worsted him.
It was The Destiny that brought him home
Without the Spanish gold.— O, he was wrong,
But such a wrong, in Gloriana's day,
Was more than right, was immortality.
He had just half an hour to put all this
Into his pipe and smoke it.—

                    The red fire,
The red heroic fire that filled his veins
When the proud flag of England floated out
Its challenge to the world — all gone to ash?
What! Was the great red wine that Drake had quaffed
Vinegar? He must fawn, haul down his flag,
And count all nations nobler than his own,
Tear out the lions from the painted shields
That hung his poop, for fear that he offend
The pride of Spain? Treason to sack the ships
Of Spain? The wounds of slaughtered Englishmen
Cried out — *there is no law beyond the line!*
Treason to sweep the seas with Francis Drake?
Treason to fight for England?

                        If it were so,
The times had changed and quickly. He had been
A school-boy in the morning of the world
Playing with wooden swords and winning crowns
Of tinsel; but his comrades had out-grown
Their morning-game, and gathered round to mock
His battles in the sunset. Yet he knew

[224]

That all his life had passed in that brief day;
And he was old, too old to understand
The smile upon the face of Buckingham,
The smile on Cobham's face, at that great word
England!

        He knew the solid earth was changed
To something less than dust among the stars —
And, O, be sure he knew that he was wrong,
That gleams would come,
Gleams of a happier world for younger men,
That Commonwealth, far off. This was a time
Of sadder things, destruction of the old
Before the new was born. At least he knew
It was his own way that had brought the world
Thus far, England thus far! How could he change,
Who had loved England as a man might love
His mistress, change from year to fickle year?
For the new years would change, even as the old.
No — he was wedded to that old first love,
Crude flesh and blood, and coarse as meat and drink,
The woman — England; no fine angel-isle,
Ruled by that male Salome — Buckingham!
Better the axe than to live on and wage
These new and silent and more deadly wars
That play at friendship with our enemies.
Such times are evil. Not of their own desire
They lead to good, blind agents of that Hand
Which now had hewed him down, down to his knees,
But in a prouder battle than men knew.

His pipe was out, the guard was at the door.

Raleigh was not a god. But, when he climbed
The scaffold, I believe he looked a man.
And when the axe fell, I believe that God
Set on his shoulders that immortal head
Which he desired on earth.

      O, he was wrong!
But when that axe fell, not one shout was raised.
That mighty throng around that crimson block
Stood silent — like the hushed black cloud that holds
The thunder. You might hear the headsman's breath.
Stillness like that is dangerous, being charged,
Sometimes, with thought, Sir Lewis! England sleeps!
What if, one day, the Stewart should be called
To know that England wakes? What if a shout
Should thunder-strike Whitehall, and the dogs lift
Their heads along the fringes of the crowd
To catch a certain savour that I know,
The smell of blood and saw-dust? —

        Ah, Sir Lewis,

'Tis hard to find one little seed of right
Among so many wrongs. Raleigh was wrong,
And yet — it was because he loved his country
Next to himself, Sir Lewis, by your leave,
His country butchered him. You did not know
That I was only third in his affections?
The night I told him — we were parting then —
I had begged the last disposal of his body,
Did he not say, with O, so gentle a smile,
' Thou hadst not always the disposal of it
In life, dear Bess. 'Tis well it should be thine
In death!' "

[226]

      " The jest was bitter at such an hour,
And somewhat coarse in grain," Stukeley replied.
" Indeed I thought him kinder."

                              " Kinder," she said,
Laughing bitterly.

                    Stukeley looked at her.
She whispered something, and his lewd old eyes
Fastened upon her own. He knelt by her.
" Perhaps," he said, " your woman's wit has found
A better way to solve this bitter business."
Her head moved on the pillow with little tossings.
He touched her hand. It leapt quickly away.
She hugged that strange white bundle to her breast,
And writhed back, smiling at him, across the bed.

" Ah, Bess," he whispered huskily, pressing his lips
To that warm hollow where her head had lain,
" There is one way to close the long dispute,
Keep the estates unbroken in your hands
And stop all slanderous tongues, one happy way.
We have some years to live; and why alone?"
" Alone?" she sighed. " My husband thought of that.
He wrote a letter to me, long ago,
When he was first condemned. He said — he said —
Now let me think — what was it that he said? —
I had it all by heart. Beseech you, Bess,
Hide not yourself for many days, he said."
" True wisdom that," quoth Stukeley, " for the love
That seeks to chain the living to the dead
Is but self-love at best!"

                  " And yet," she said,
" How his poor heart was torn between two cares,
Love of himself and care for me, as thus:
Love God! Begin to repose yourself on Him!
Therein you shall find true and lasting riches;
But all the rest is nothing. When you have tired
Your thoughts on earthly things, when you have travelled
Through all the glittering pomps of this proud world
You shall sit down by Sorrow in the end.
Begin betimes, and teach your little son
To serve and fear God also.
Then God will be a husband unto you,
And unto him a father: nor can Death
Bereave you any more. When I am gone,
No doubt you shall be sought unto by many
For the world thinks that I was very rich.
No greater misery can befall you, Bess,
Than to become a prey, and, afterwards,
To be despised."

                  " Human enough," said Stukeley,
" And yet — self-love, self-love ! "

                        " Ah no," quoth she,
" You have not heard the end: *God knows, I speak it*
Not to dissuade you — not to dissuade you, mark —
From marriage. That will be the best for you,
Both in respect of God and of the world.
Was *that* self-love, Sir Lewis? Ah, not all.
And thus he ended: *For his father's sake*
That chose and loved you in his happiest times,
Remember your poor child! The Everlasting,
Infinite, powerful, and inscrutable God,

Keep you and yours, have mercy upon me,
And teach me to forgive my false accusers —
Wrong, even in death, you see. Then — *My true wife,*
Farewell!
Bless my poor boy! Pray for me! My true God,
Hold you both in His arms, both in His arms!
I know that he was wrong. You did not know,
Sir Lewis, that he had left me a little child.
Come closer. You shall see its orphaned face,
The sad, sad relict of a man that loved
His country — all that's left to me. Come, look!"
She beckoned Stukeley nearer. He bent down
Curiously. Her feverish fingers drew
The white wrap from the bundle in her arms,
And, with a smile that would make angels weep,
She showed him, pressed against her naked breast,
Terrible as Medusa, the grey flesh
And shrivelled face, embalmed, the thing that dropped
Into the headsman's basket, months agone,—
The head of Raleigh.

                Half her body lay
Bare, while she held that grey babe to her heart;
But Judas hid his face. . . .
"Living," she said, "he was not always mine;
But — dead — I shall not wean him" —

                      Then, I too
Covered my face — I cannot tell you more.
There was a dreadful silence in that room,
Silence that, as I know, shattered the brain
Of Stukeley. — When I dared to raise my head
Beneath that silent thunder of our God,

The man had gone —
                        This is his letter, sirs,
Written from Lundy Island: *For God's love,*
Tell them it is a cruel thing to say
That I drink blood. I have no secret sin.
A thousand pound is not so great a sum;
And that is all they paid me, every penny.
Salt water, that is all the drink I taste
On this rough island. Somebody has taught
The sea-gulls how to wail around my hut
All night, like lost souls. And there is a face,
A dead man's face that laughs in every storm,
And sleeps in every pool along the coast.
I thought it was my own, once. But I know
These actions never, never, on God's earth,
Will turn out to their credit, who believe
That I drink blood.
                        He crumpled up the letter
And tossed it into the fire.
                        "Galen," said Ben,
"I think you are right — that one should pity villains."

.   .   .   .

The clock struck twelve. The bells began to peal.
We drank a cup of sack to the New Year.
"New songs, new voices, all as fresh as may,"
Said Ben to Brome, "but I shall never live
To hear them."
                        All was not so well, indeed,
With Ben, as hitherto. Age had come upon him.
He dragged one foot as in paralysis.
The critics bayed against the old lion, now,

And called him arrogant. " My brain," he said,
" Is yet unhurt although, set round with pain,
It cannot long hold out." He never stooped,
Never once pandered to that brainless hour.
His coat was thread-bare. Weeks had passed of late
Without his voice resounding in our inn.

" The statues are defiled, the gods dethroned,
The Ionian movement reigns, not the free soul.
And, as for me, I have lived too long," he said.
" Well — I can weave the old threnodies anew."
And, filling his cup, he murmured, soft and low,
A new song, breaking on an ancient shore:

I

Marlowe is dead, and Greene is in his grave,
   And sweet Will Shakespeare long ago is gone!
Our Ocean-shepherd sleeps beneath the wave;
Robin is dead, and Marlowe in his grave.
Why should I stay to chant an idle stave,
   And in my Mermaid Tavern drink alone?
For Kit is dead and Greene is in his grave,
   And sweet Will Shakespeare long ago is gone.

II

Where is the singer of the Faërie Queen?
   Where are the lyric lips of Astrophel?
Long, long ago, their quiet graves were green;
Ay, and the grave, too, of their Faërie Queen!
And yet their faces, hovering here unseen,

Call me to taste their new-found œnomel;
To sup with him who sang the Faërie Queen;
To drink with him whose name was Astrophel.

III

I drink to that great Inn beyond the grave!
   —If there be none, the gods have done us wrong.—
Ere long I hope to chant a better stave,
In some great Mermaid Inn beyond the grave;
And quaff the best of earth that heaven can save,
   Red wine like blood, deep love of friends and song.
I drink to that great Inn beyond the grave;
   And hope to greet my golden lads ere long.

He raised his cup and drank in silence. Brome
Drank with him, too. The bells had ceased to peal.
Galen shook hands, and bade us all good night.
Then Brome, a little wistfully, I thought,
Looked at his old-time master, and prepared
To follow.
            "Good night — Ben," he said, a pause
Before he spoke the name. "Good night! Good night!
My dear old Brome," said Ben.
                          And, at the door,
Brome whispered to me, "He is lonely now.
There are not many left of his old friends.
We all go out — like this — into the night.
But what a fleet of stars!" he said, and shook
My hand, and smiled, and pointed to the sky.

And, when I looked into the room again,
The lights were very dim, and I believed
That Ben had fallen asleep. His great grey head
Was bowed across the table, on his arms.
Then, all at once, I knew that he was weeping;
And like a shadow I crept back again,
And stole into the night.

                There as I stood
Under the painted sign, I could have vowed
That I, too, heard the voices of the dead,
The voices of his old companions,
Gathering round him in that lonely room,
Till all the timbers of the Mermaid Inn
Trembled above me with their ghostly song:

I

    Say to the King, quoth Raleigh
      I have a tale to tell him,
        Wealth beyond derision,
          Veils to lift from the sky,
    Seas to sail for England
      And a little dream to sell him,—
        Gold, the gold of a vision,
          That angels cannot buy.

II

    Fair thro' the walls of his dungeon,
      — What were the stones but a shadow? —
      Streamed the light of the rapture,
        The lure that he followed of old,

The dream of his old companions,
The vision of El Dorado,
The fleet that they never could capture,
The City of Sunset-gold.

III

Yet did they sail the seas
And, dazed with exceeding wonder,
Straight through the sunset-glory
Plunge into the dawn:
Leaving their home behind them,
By a road of splendour and thunder,
They came to their home in amazement
Simply by sailing on.

THE END